TALES OUT OF CLASS

TALES
OUT OF
CLASS

The chronicles of a primary school teacher

Steve Eddison

Copyright © 2025 Steve Eddison

The moral right of the author has been asserted.

Apart from any fair dealing for the purposes of research or private study, or criticism or review, as permitted under the Copyright, Designs and Patents Act 1988, this publication may only be reproduced, stored or transmitted, in any form or by any means, with the prior permission in writing of the publishers, or in the case of reprographic reproduction in accordance with the terms of licences issued by the Copyright Licensing Agency. Enquiries concerning reproduction outside those terms should be sent to the publishers.

Troubador Publishing Ltd
Unit E2 Airfield Business Park
Harrison Road, Market Harborough
Leicestershire LE16 7UL
Tel: 0116 279 2299
Email: books@troubador.co.uk
Web: www.troubador.co.uk

ISBN 978-1-83628-272-3

British Library Cataloguing in Publication Data.
A catalogue record for this book is available from the British Library.

The manufacturer's authorised representative in the EU for product safety is Authorised Rep Compliance Ltd, 71 Lower Baggot Street, Dublin D02 P593 Ireland (www.arccompliance.com).

Printed and bound by CPI Group (UK) Ltd, Croydon, CR0 4YY
Typeset in 11pt Minion Pro by Troubador Publishing Ltd, Leicester, UK

For services above and beyond the call of kinship, I hereby award one Marvellous Mother Merit to the first Mrs Eddison and one Super Spouse Sticker to the second.

Contents

Introduction		ix
Part One	Autumn is the cruellest term	1
Part Two	Midwinter spring is its own term	79
Part Three	Summer term views	151
Part Four	And breathe…	217
A short plenary		264

Introduction

Once upon a time a newly qualified teacher looked out upon his first ever class. He was on a mission to save the world. A short time later he found he was also on a mission to survive till home time. His discovery that the only certainty in teaching is that nothing is certain was a game changer. Suddenly he knew teaching wasn't an exact science and that even the best laid lesson plans oft go awry. In the blink of an evil eye contact between Taylor and Britney, or the photocopier getting jammed or Harrison throwing up over Ahmed's interpretation of Van Gogh's Sunflowers, a teacher's world (or at least his classroom) can be literally turned upside down.

As these tales demonstrate, what happens in a lesson plan does not always happen in a classroom. But then that's what makes the job of teaching what it is: scary, exhausting, funny, irritating, satisfying, hilarious, draining, distressing, entertaining, sad and rewarding. And because, where thirty children are concerned, you can experience all of these emotions and more in the space of ten minutes, there's never a dull moment.

Although I have little to compare it with (I tried engineering once only to find mechanical things hate me) I can honestly say that teaching is the best job in the world. So, to the children who hung on my every word (and the vast majority of them that didn't) but who together conspired to make me chronicle my life in the classroom, I offer my heartfelt thanks and my sincere apologies.

Tales out of Class is a collection of some of my favourite TES columns. In order to put chaos into some kind of order (a way of life for primary practitioners) I have divided it into four familiar sections: three frenetic terms followed by a long summer break.

Part One

Autumn is the cruellest term

1

Dear School Diary... what chaos will this year bring?

15th September 2017

Dear School Diary,

You are a pristine place where no man has set biro. An anthology of emptiness where no scribbled engagements lurk and where the future is yet to be determined. In your pages destiny remains unwritten and my event horizon is empty. For now at least, I can flick through time and enjoy its brand new smell.

No ordinary diary can comply with the natural order of a teacher's life. I can't even contemplate a world that begins in the bleak landscape that is January. We all know that long before autumn term is over the months beyond will have been turned into a ruined landscape of pencillings in and crossings out. A tangle of rearranged rendezvous, cancelled engagements and unlikely deadlines.

Dear School Diary,

By the start of next term the crush of obligations will threaten to overwhelm your remaining pages. By the time the fairy lights have been returned to the loft, we'll be back in education's fast lane. Reckless assignations and perilous appointments will speed towards us. New dates will jostle with old dates, like cyclists in a packed peloton, each vying for prime position in the long sprint towards summer.

The year end is August's rightful place. An alternative dimension in time and space. A no-child's land of blissful unawareness, entirely separate from the reality that begins in September and ends in July. In the chronicle of school events August is a sacred place where I will write in capitals, using a fat marker pen, one word followed by several exclamation marks. HOLIDAYS!!!!!

Dear School Diary,

Today is the first staff meeting of the year. It is an event that will begin with the ritual gathering together of teachers who can't quite believe the summer break is over. In the childless hinterland that is education's New Year's Eve, most staff will still be in holiday mode. They will swan around in jeans and suntans and sow the first crop of congealing coffee mugs on window ledges and shelves while they go in search of display paper and a staple gun.

Very soon now, Ms Boudicca will call us together and display her proposed itinerary for our annual attempt to raise academic standards and keep one step ahead of Ofsted. At this point teachers will gaze mournfully at a banner that reads, Some Key Dates for your Diary, and wonder if her use of comic sans is meant to be ironic.

Of course I could access these dates electronically, but I prefer the future to be handwritten. Like a child with a new work book and a misguided sense of optimism, I will begin by making careful notes of important dates ... Professional Development Training Days, Target Setting Meetings, Special Educational Needs Reviews, Parents' Evenings, Book Scrutiny Dates, Superheroes Week...

Dear School Diary,
Time is no longer on my side. I have conflicting commitments in mid-October ... My amendments need amending ... My writing is losing the will to remain legible ... A coffee stain has appeared in the middle of Week 4 ...

Dear School Diary,
For the misuse you are about to receive, please accept my sincere apologies.

Autumn is the cruellest term

2

Living the dream

12th September 2014

For two hours I experiment with changing my body position. I lie on my right side. I lie on my left side. I lie on my back. I try re-plumping my pillow and re-positioning the duvet. As a last resort I heave several weary sighs that I hope won't wake my wife up.

'It's just nervous excitement,' she mumbles. 'Try to relax.'

Eventually I fall into a fitful sleep that sees me wrestling with the fiendishly intractable problem of how to access and complete the new electronic dinner register. I switch the alarm off half an hour before it was due to wake me up anyway and take a shower.

I never sleep properly the night before the first day back at school. After all these years my stomach still churns in anticipation of a new class. While my bowl of cereal quietly congeals I consider my options; what's the worst that could happen if I never went back? Then the prospect of watching daytime TV for the rest of my life forces me to roll up my sleeves and steel myself for the year ahead.

My fears turn out to be unfounded. The first day back is characterised by good order. The children arrive neatly packaged in new uniforms with scrubbed faces and tidy haircuts. Even Hayley, who normally looks like a Victorian street urchin ten seconds after reaching the school gates, seems resistant to wear and tear. For the first time ever she gets to lunchtime with her plaits intact, her tie in place and no signs of marker pen on her clothes or skin.

And it's not just appearances that make the day go smoothly. This is a fresh start and everybody is out to impress. Rules are followed meticulously and instructions are carried out to the letter. In truth it's all very unnerving. Even Jake, who comes with a history of anger management problems and a reputation for creating havoc second only to Genghis Khan's, smiles up at me like butter wouldn't melt in his mouth.

I smile back cautiously and double sticker him for good behaviour. Perhaps it's the exhaustion kicking in but I have the curious notion that this is all a dream. It's like finding myself in a meadow, with a spring in my step, a song in my heart and a growing realisation that actually it's not a meadow after all; it's a minefield. And inside my head someone is screaming at me to wake up and smell the cordite.

By mid-afternoon the strains are beginning to show. A thrown pencil and a minor argument that ends in tears leave me feeling reassured that it won't be long before things are back to normal. I smile to think that in the not too distant future Jake will swear at me and storm out onto the corridor. I sigh in the knowledge that within a week Hayley will lose her tie and go home looking like she's been dragged through a hedge backwards.

'So how was your first day at school?' asks my wife as we turn in for the night.

'Zzzzzzzzzzzzz,' I reply.

Autumn is the cruellest term

3

We fix classrooms up and dust pupils down

7th September 2018

I'm waiting for someone to get so fed up of hearing the buzzer they'll raise the barrier and let me into the car park. After five unsuccessful attempts I spot Aleesha on the opposite side of the road. She is carrying something large and red under her arm. The nearer she gets to me the more incredulous I become. She spots me and comes across to say hello.

'Don't build your hopes up,' I tell her but she only looks confused. The intense summer heat-wave might be a thing of the past but the air temperature is still mid-twenties. I point to a sky that is anything but threatening and say, 'I reckon the chance of a freak blizzard is pretty much out of the question.' Her expression remains the same. I remind myself that primary teachers should avoid being cryptic. 'What are you doing with that sledge?' I ask.

A minute later Mrs Rottweiler interrupts us. Getting into school is not as easy as it used to be before they invented safeguarding and it's harder still when your electronic fob has temporarily misplaced itself. Her voice over the intercom sounds testier than normal. 'Who is it?' she says

'George Clooney,' I reply.

'Where's your fob, Mr Eddison?' she asks. But before I can think of a witty innuendo she says, 'Actually, don't bother. Life's too short.' The barrier opens and I drive inside.

It's the week before term starts and my younger colleagues have been hard at work. Classrooms that a few short weeks ago resembled disaster zones have been transformed into havens of enlightenment. Where there were barren pin boards, pocked with shreds of old backing paper and stubborn staples, new and stimulating learning walls have flourished.

Miss Brightside smiles a wan smile that makes me wonder when she last saw daylight. Her displays are bright and colourful, her reading corner reminds me of a trendy children's bookshop and I have to negotiate a tropical rainforest just to get to her table. Battling my way through trailing greenery teeming with monkeys, snakes, parrots and giant insects, I can't help but think I ought to be wearing mosquito repellent.

'Looks like you're all ready for your new class,' I tell Miss Brightside, who in turn sighs and admits to being uncertain. Eight times she's reconfigured her tables and she's still not sure where to sit Jarrod in relation to those children (nearly everybody) he finds it difficult to get on with. I smile reassuringly. 'He'll be too engaged with your Rainforest Topic to worry about banging somebody out,' I tell her.

While we both know this isn't true, we also know that it's important to remain positive. Over the next year there will be endless repairs to carry out. Displays will be damaged, resources will get trashed and children will be in constant need of TLC. But then that's what primary teachers do, isn't it? They fix classrooms up, dust children down and start all over again.

'You can never have too much optimism,' I tell Miss Brightside. 'Aleesha thinks finding an old plastic sledge in a skip is a sign it's going to snow.'

Autumn is the cruellest term

4

A sting in the tail

20th September 2013

I love these early September afternoons when the weather thinks it's still summer and my children don't yet know I'm a soft touch. Having a new class who follow rules and hang on your every word makes this the best time to be a teacher. If only things were always this calm and relaxed.

Angelica is the first to twitch. A moment later the spiky-haired boy sitting next to her – whose name I am struggling to remember – is doing the same. The truth dawns when Jennifer who sits opposite them suddenly leaps to her feet and flails ineffectively at some invisible assailant. *Vespula Vulgaris* has infiltrated our classroom with a determination to wreak educational havoc. Panic ensues with pandemonium snapping at its heels.

Suddenly I feel like the U.N. in the middle of a world crisis. This is because before I get the chance to negotiate a peace settlement the warlike Harry has assumed leadership and taken unilateral action on everybody's behalf. Armed to the teeth with his RE folder he charges into the thick of it (wherever the thick of it might be). He swashes to the left and buckles to the right before roaring at Jennifer to keep still. 'It's on your back. I can get it if you keep still,' he tells her.

Jennifer's flight response kicks in and she runs for cover in the book corner. Harry is not to be deterred however and keeping faith in his RE folder sets off in pursuit. By now he is intent on smiting anything in his path.

My appeals for calm eventually penetrate the chaos and shock a critical mass of children into a watchful silence. A fragile ceasefire is declared. Harry grudgingly lowers his RE folder. 'But it's a wasp, Mr Eddison,' he protests.

'I can see what it is,' I tell him, although in fairness I can't. I can only gauge its location at any given moment by observing the flinching of those it gets close to. 'And if we want to avoid anybody getting stung by the wasp I suggest we keep as still as we can until it finds its way out of the window.'

'I think we should kill it to be on the safe side,' says Harry.

'If you ignore it, it will ignore you,' I explain, only to be undermined by the fact that it isn't ignoring the boy whose name I can't remember. For some reason it is fascinated by the gel used to spike his hair. We wait calmly while it investigates the unusual topography of his head. Only Harry is visibly agitated.

Eventually the insect gets bored and after one more circuit of the classroom disappears. Assuming it must have drifted out through the open window I relax. 'There you are,

Harry,' I say. 'All you have to do with wasps is stay calm. Don't threaten them and they won't threaten you.'

'But my dad says they were only put on this earth to annoy and sting people,' he replies. 'They don't have any uses and should be wiped out completely.'

I leap to their defence. 'Well maybe you should tell your dad that the common wasp – Latin name *Vespula Vulgaris* – is an essential part of our eco-system, and without it we would be overrun with flies and other pests that damage crops and spread disease. He should also know that wasps have no desire whatsoever to sting humans.'

That is unless you accidentally rest your bare arm on the one crawling across your table.

I shriek something in Latin and it isn't *Vespula Vulgaris*.

Autumn is the cruellest term

5

The art of conker warfare

28th October 2016

Today I am a battlefield commander, pacing the classroom in anticipation of giving the order to go over the top. But first I must brief my platoon on the dangers that lie ahead. 'Right, kids, switch off those tablet computers and listen carefully. There will be no more virtual learning on my watch. The time has come for you to interface with the real world. To risk life, limb and eyesight in the pursuit of a practical education.'

With their minds smartly at attention, I explain that our *Forces Project* is a perilous one. There will be no tapping icons and watching electrons dance across a screen. (The educational equivalent of using remotely controlled drones to deliver laser-guided death from an RAF base in Lincolnshire.) Today's learning will be close up and personal. Armed only with raw courage and a modicum of protective clothing they will do battle with autumn's weapons of ultimate destruction.

I take out my carrier bag and empty its contents onto the carpet. Tens of shiny brown nuts roll around the floor. The reactions of the children are varied. They range from total confusion to utter disappointment. I ask if anyone knows what they are. Three failed attempts later, James tells me they're conkers. He also explains that their proper name is horse chestnuts and that unlike sweet chestnuts you can't eat them because they're poisonous.

When I ask which children have played conkers the response is equally discouraging. The popularity of a playground sport enjoyed by countless children during the twentieth century is hanging by a thread in the twenty first; battered into submission by the all-conquering microchip. Gathering nuts in a damp woods and whacking them at each other can't compete with a PlayStation Vita, while worries about developing RSI (Repetitive Swiping Injury) are tiny compared to the threat of getting Bruised Knuckle Syndrome.

But is the demise of conkers a sign of the times or are more sinister forces at work? I have it on good authority (a bloke in the pub) that there are those who would wrap such games in bio-degradable lavatory paper and flush them down the composting toilet of history. According to the Law of Diminishing Sobriety, our nanny state has teamed up with opportunistic litigators to rid the world of the simple pleasures of a bygone age.

So will conkers go the way of all the great character building activities of the twentieth century? The wearing of leg braces after contracting polio? Having your ringworm irradiated? Doing PE in your vest and pants? Not while I'm around it won't. The risk assessment is signed and the permission slips are gathered in. The children don their hard hats, their safety glasses and their leather gardening gauntlets, and take up arms. It's time to let battle commence.

Overcoming the fear of causing injury by reckless teaching is a tough nut to crack. But someone has to do it. Someone has to laugh in the face of danger; scoff at cowardliness; put two fingers up to the grey merchants of health and safety; sneer at... *'Oh my God! Daniel, stop eating that conker! Spit it out! Now!'*

Autumn is the cruellest term

6

Crime and punishment

19th December 2014

'Why is there a child crying in the disabled toilet?' says Ms Boudicca. The noise subsides as everyone turns to look in my direction. The sound of distress that a moment earlier was no more than an annoying component of the general clamour is suddenly the focus of everyone's attention.

By the time the little girl is released a crowd has gathered. People are muttering their disbelief and pointing the finger of blame at me. If this was the Wild West they would have me strung up from the nearest tree. My excuses... *I never heard her... I was busy... I thought somebody was dealing with it...* are the pathetic pleadings of a guilty man.

To make matters worse our headteacher, Ms Boudicca, insists on clutching the sobbing infant to her maternal bosom. 'There, there, sweetheart, you're safe now,' she soothes. 'He's a very naughty Mr Eddison, isn't he? Leaving you locked in the toilet like that.' She gives me the sort of look my wife gives me when she arrives home in the pouring rain to find Sky Sports has taken precedence over getting the washing in.

However, before anyone rushes to judgement it is important to examine the facts. It was 8.40am and our school entrance area (where the disabled toilet is situated) was like a mining town during the California Gold Rush. All human emotion was on display and sounds of distress – *blubbing children distraught at having to come to school; weeping parents whose lives are falling apart; sobbing teachers tormented by upcoming lesson observations* – were just part of the general hubbub.

Under these circumstances the anguish of one small child locked in a lavatory is easy to overlook. Especially by someone who has other things on his mind. I am working in our integrated resource today and was sent to meet the students who arrive by taxi. We greeted each other excitedly. There was much whooping and sharing of high fives. And that was just with the taxi driver who was overjoyed that I'd come to take them off his hands.

But exchanging greetings was only a part of my remit. I was also required to make mental notes about the children's behaviour; absorb important messages from parents and carers; collect and record medications; and reunite lunchboxes with owners. Too many responsibilities, perhaps, for someone who by his own admission is not gifted in the art of multi-tasking?

Taking all this into account is it not proved beyond reasonable doubt that I am an innocent teacher? That I am a man more sinned against than sinning? And that my only crime was one of being in the wrong place at the wrong time?

When I get home from school I complain to my wife about the injustice I have suffered at the hands of Ms Boudicca, but for some reason she isn't listening. 'Did you hear what I just said?' I ask, but she fails to respond. Instead she stares through the window at her sodden washing. And I catch that look in her eye. It is reminiscent of someone contemplating a lynching.

Autumn is the cruellest term

7

High-wire act

13th December 2013

Late-night voices raised in anger, drunkenness or fear rarely disturb Caleb. He sleeps on indifferent to the sounds of horror, porn and hip hop. Not even breaking bottles, barking dogs, howling alarms, slamming doors or squealing tyres wake him up. The throb of the police helicopter is the soundtrack to his dreams.

But he cannot sleep through the sound of this night. It scares him more than the things he did earlier when he stood on a platform eight metres from the ground. 'Now I want you to hold onto the rope above your head and place your left foot on the cable,' said Jackie. Caleb, who has some trust issues, voiced his opinion that our instructor was off her head. Jackie remained unruffled. 'Come on, Caleb, you can do it,' she insisted.

With the whole of Team Hedgehog behind him, urging him on, he took a tentative leap of faith. One foot felt its way onto the cable, followed by the other. Gripping the rope tightly, he eased himself out over the dizzying drop. Then just as he began to make his way along Nathan yelled out, 'Look, he's doing it!' And like Peter on the Sea of Galilee, Caleb's faith went from under him and he fell.

He didn't fall far. An instant later the safety harness dug into his thighs. For a moment he dangled in mid-air, scrabbling for purchase. Then his feet regained the cable and his hand grabbed the rope. Fifteen minutes later he completed the course and we nicknamed him Indiana Jones.

The High Ropes is one of several challenging activities on offer at this outdoor education centre near Bakewell in Derbyshire's Peak District. Before bedtime Caleb has helped build a den in the forest and crouched inside it while it was tested with a bucket of ice cold water. He has crawled through underground plastic tunnels to escape a giant child-eating spider and completed a death-defying obstacle course through the Amazon Jungle. And after dark he bravely followed a rope that wound mysteriously through bear-infested woods.

During the day Team Hedgehog readily accept Caleb's learning and behavioural difficulties and support him in every way they can. By bedtime, however, tiredness has set in and tempers are getting frayed. 'The rest of Team Hedgehog do not want you to throw your dirty socks at them, whip them with your towel or pull their duvets off and stuff them through the window,' I explain to Caleb. It is my umpteenth visit to his dormitory.

Undertaking challenging activities and working as a team are only part of the residential experience. Being away from home for a few nights and sharing a room with five other children is a key part of it too. And this bit is a lot more demanding than balancing on a cable eight metres above ground.

After lengthy negotiations the rules and boundaries of bedtime behaviour are re-established and I return to my book and chair that have been placed strategically just outside the door. Ten minutes pass and most of the children have settled down. One by one their whispers die out as they drift off to sleep. Soon it is silent. Or almost silent.

I put my ear against the door. Someone is sobbing. I creep inside and find Caleb awake. 'What's the matter?' I ask.

'I don't like the noise,' he says.

Apart from the gentle breathing of Team Hedgehog there is only the overwhelming silence of the night.

'I can't hear anything,' I whisper.

'I know, that's what I'm scared of,' he replies.

Autumn is the cruellest term

8

Is the playground heading for bigly war? Sad!

13th October 2017

There is tension in the air. Trouble is brewing. We live in dangerous times. In a remote corner of the playground, Big Donald (not his real name), is waving a very large stick around and declaring to the world that he has every intention of using it to devastating effect. Little Kim (also not his real name) is undeterred. He too is armed with a stick (albeit of much smaller proportions) and is threatening to whack Big Donald in the nuts. The situation is getting out of hand.

Because Big Donald has anger management issues, most children go out of their way (or rather *his*) to avoid him. Others generally defer to his requests to borrow their footballs, twirl their fidget spinners and take their place in the dinner queue. One small group has a more symbiotic relationship with him. It's useful to have a powerful friend, even if he does sometimes get you in a headlock and knuckle your skull.

It would be useful, in terms of promoting social cohesion, if Little Kim fitted into one of the above categories, but he doesn't. And to make matters worse – like Albert Ramsbottom, in Stanley Holloway's famous monologue – he is the sort of boy who can't help poking dangerous things with a stick. He has no idea that there are three things in life you should never poke: a lion, a wasps' nest and a large person with a short fuse.

The mother of all playground battles is only avoided thanks to the quick thinking of Tamara. Realising the situation had already progressed beyond the point where her Peer Mediator training might help resolve it, she followed protocol to the letter and reported it to a teacher. And not just any teacher, but the one most qualified to intervene.

Mrs Sensible, is vastly experienced in the art of defusing hostile situations. She has been the still centre at many a stormy playground dispute and takes no chances. She approaches with caution. She makes an assessment. She recognises that any over-authoritarian demand for an immediate ceasefire will be counter-productive. Maintaining a calm head and using her most reassuring voice, she gradually imposes her authority. Both sides stop shouting threats, put down their tree parts and contemplate her road map to peace.

Big Donald and Little Kim listen in silence as they are taught how to avoid future confrontations. They learn why it is important to adopt more grown-up negotiation techniques to resolve disputes. How it is vital to practise skills such as:

'*Ignoring provocative remarks*', '*calming down by counting to ten*' and '*not using the school garden as an armoury.*' After a cooling-off period the combatants grudgingly apologise, briefly shake hands and reluctantly retire to separate areas of the playground.

The problem with Big Donald and Little Kim is that they are emotionally immature. They can't control their feelings. They're incapable of dealing with anger, and when aroused find it difficult to exercise any form of self-restraint. Actually, it's a good job they only have access to sticks and stones. Heaven knows what would happen in they got their hands on weapons of mass destruction.

Autumn is the cruellest term

9

Dawn of the dead hamster

27th November 2015

'What about zombies?' says Rogan. 'Zombies are dead and they come back to life, don't they, Mr Eddison?' I'm not entirely sure how this discussion lurched in the direction of the un-dead. We were supposed to be helping James. He is upset after his Uncle Ben died at the wheel in the early hours of this morning.

It takes me a while to work out that Uncle Ben is (or rather was) a golden hamster. 'The death of a much loved family pet can be traumatic,' I tell his mum. 'But we'll start the day with a special circle time to help him come to terms with the loss. Lots of children will have had pets that have died. I'll get them to talk about their experiences to show that he's not on his own.'

Our class conversation proceeds as smoothly as a funeral cortege until Bradley describes the events surrounding the death of Captain Nemo. One morning he discovered the bloated body of his beloved goldfish floating upside down on the top of his bowl. A funeral service was rejected, presumably on the grounds that it might prove too harrowing. Instead his step-dad fished him out with an egg slice and flushed him unceremoniously to his final resting place in the sewers of Sheffield.

For some reason Bradley's story leaves James more upset than ever. It isn't until Lucy tells us how her cat, Sooty, had to be *put to sleep* that he finally stops sobbing and becomes interested in the discussion. The term *put to sleep* is causing some confusion. Rogan and Nathan soon engage in an intense philosophical debate about it. This in turn raises the spectre of the un-dead.

'Sleep is the same as being dead, isn't it, Mr Eddison?' says Rogan.

'No it's not, cos when you're dead you don't wake up,' argues Nathan.

'I don't mean *that* dead,' snaps Rogan. And the argument gets increasingly acrimonious until…

'My Rabbit died and he woke up again,' says Amelia. Now everyone is listening. Amelia does not enter class discussions lightly. Neither does she fantasise or tell whoppers. 'A dog jumped into his run. And when my dad got it out he was dead. So we put him in a cardboard box in the garage and we were going to bury him the next day. And when my dad opened the garage he heard a noise. And when he looked in the box my rabbit was alive again.'

I smile and tell Amelia that her rabbit only appeared

to be dead. He was temporarily paralysed by fear. During the night he must have woken up from his trance. 'So could Uncle Ben wake up?' asks James. His voice trembles with hope and I want to yes. But then you can't shield children from cold hard facts forever.

The truth hurts and James is inconsolable until it gets to home time. That's when a newly resurrected and oddly shrunken looking Uncle Ben arrives to meet him. His mum gives me a huge wink. 'Turns out he wasn't dead after all, Mr Eddison. He was just asleep.'

Autumn is the cruellest term

10

Washing with dinosaurs

10th October 2014

Despite an escaped tyrannosaurus rex rampaging through its inner workings our washing machine has survived unscathed. 'It got into the sump and stopped the water from draining out,' says the repairman. He places the offending dinosaur into my safe keeping and wipes his hands. 'You're lucky it didn't get wedged between the drum and the tank. It would have caused absolute carnage in there.'

I can see the headline now – *Tyrannosaurus Wrecks Washer* – only it's not a real dinosaur. It's a representation pressed onto a disc the size of a two pence coin. 'A theme park souvenir I took from a child,' I tell the repairman. He gives me a curious look. 'He was playing with it when he should have been doing SPAG.' His curiosity turns to alarm. 'Spelling, punctuation and grammar,' I explain.

James is gifted and talented in dinosaurs. And he especially likes sharing his knowledge with the only person he knows who might actually date from the Upper Cretaceous. When I recently kept him behind to discuss the unexpected appearance of a brontosaurus in assembly, he assumed it was because I was eager to learn how palaeontologists have recently discovered the fossilised bones of a titanosaur that would have weighed more than fourteen African elephants.

I am doing my best to make James's dinosaurs extinct. A velociraptor, an allosaurus, a diplodocus, a brachiosaurus, two iguanodons, a triceratops and an inflatable stegosaurus with a slow puncture have been catastrophically wiped out and left to fossilise in my drawer. How this particular tyrannosaur ended up in our washing machine is a complete mystery. Well almost.

Since teaching part time I have been encouraged to extend my domestic repertoire. This now includes doing the washing without supervision. It is a leap of faith on my wife's part. Household appliances don't respond well to pleading, cursing, kicking or having their parenthood questioned. And my previous track record with the dishwasher isn't good. My ability to stack efficiently and to use rinse aid effectively have been judged inadequate on more than one occasion.

My failure to meet the required standards for operating the washing machine should therefore have come as no surprise. Twice I have turned essentially white items into mainly pink items by not spotting a distinctly red item amongst the non-coloureds. But my main area for improvement is in checking pockets. Removing tiny bits of tissue paper from dark clothing with a roll of sticky tape is a laborious task that I am told could easily be avoided.

Clearly my wife does not understand the mystical properties of men's trousers. No matter how carefully we remove every item from our pockets there is always something left over. Usually it's a tissue. Occasionally – and often regretfully – I have laundered money. As far as I know this is the first time I've put a theropod through the eco cycle.

My wife enters the utility room with a wash basket in tow and a determination to stay in charge of it. 'So what caused the problem?' she asks.

'A dinosaur,' says the repairman.

'Tell me something I didn't know,' she replies.

Autumn is the cruellest term

11

One too many Wonka Bars

16th October 2015

Waiting around for half a lifetime to see a doctor is bad enough. Being shunned by total strangers while you do it is frankly unacceptable. The last person to come into this already packed waiting room sat beside a highly infectious and incredibly whingeing child just to avoid sitting sit next to me. Was it my bright orange face and green hair that upset him? Or could it have been my white dungarees with stripy stockings?

Whatever the immediate cause of my social discomfort I blame the crisis in General Practice. There are just too many patients and not enough GPs. And if I'd known my appointment was going to be delayed by over thirty minutes I would have gone home first and changed into something less conspicuous. This outfit was my wife's idea. I originally planned to go as Mr Twit.

'We've had a fancy dress day at school,' I tell an old man with a severe chest infection who accidentally catches my eye between coughing spasms. 'I'm a primary teacher. I don't normally dress like this. Well only at the weekend.' The room breathes a collective sigh of relief. The old man resumes his bronchial attack. I pick up an information leaflet about testicular cancer.

Our Dahlicious Dress up Day wasn't just a *superific* way to raise money for good causes; it was a *whizz-banging* learning opportunity too. And at the end of a day packed to the gizzards with marvellous story-telling, fantastic writing and incredible drama, the children gathered for circle time. This was their chance to tell each other everything they had learned about their favourite Roald Dahl characters.

Matilda number three volunteered to be first in the hot seat. She adjusted her red ribbon, pulled up her ankle socks and began to tell the class exactly what she thought of herself. 'First of all I'm very intelligent because I have read all the books in the library. Also I have super powers to move things with my eyes and this is called telekinesis. But the best thing is that I am brave because I'm not scared of her.' She pointed her finger directly at Miss Trunchbull (aka Mrs Rottweiler).

Back in the waiting room I am half way through learning how to conduct a testicular self-examination when a thought occurs to me. Many of our children (and staff) came dressed as the characters they most resemble in real life. For example, Aaron (tallest boy in the class) came as the BFG. Shania (good at stirring up trouble) came dressed as a witch. Ms Boudicca, (head teacher and senior authority figure) came as Veruca Salt.

Just when I'm on the verge of coming up with a truly brain-boggling theory on the social psychology of fancy dress, the infectious child stops whingeing and asks, 'Mummy, why is that man dressed like a clown?' I wave away the mother's apologies and explain to the entire room that I'm an Oompa Loompa.

'Ironically I'm here to discuss my blood sugar levels,' I add. 'Diabetes is something of an occupational hazard when you work in a chocolate factory.'

Autumn is the cruellest term

12

Floodlights and tears

4th October 2013

I am wearing Miss Marsh's emerald blouse over bottle green tights. Brian Pemberton keeps telling everyone that I must be a girl because I'm wearing a dress. I keep telling him he's just jealous because he's only a tree. Eventually I stab him in his knothole with my wooden sword. Nobody messes with Merry Man 2.

There are three things I remember in detail from when I was at primary school. One was the time the caretaker caught me on the roof trying to retrieve my whirly-copter after it was forced to make an emergency landing. On that occasion Mrs Wooffet's slipper also left a lasting impression on my backside.

Another was the late winner I scored in our cup clash with Foundry Lane Juniors. The rain was driving and the pitch was a quagmire. Only seconds remained when the ball skidded across the six-yard box. Bravely I slid in between the two centre backs to meet it. The net bulged and my team mates roared. Pity it was an own goal.

But my biggest moment came when, mortally wounded, I staggered on stage and delivered those immortal lines – *The Sherriff and his men have surprised us, Robin. Maid Marion is captured and taken to Nottingham.* A moment later I died heroically in front of a packed house. My mum wept while my dad nodded stoically. Parental support is everything when you bare your soul to the world. I couldn't imagine them not being there to watch.

'One performance in a school production will outlive a thousand lessons,' I tell my drama group. This term we are doing *Much Ado About Nothing*. It will take place at a local theatre in November as part of Shakespeare Schools Festival 2013. Over the next few weeks I will tear my hair out, shout myself hoarse and model every character from Dogberry to Don Pedro.

There will be times when Signior Leonato forgets every line, when Benedick sulks in a corner and when Lady Beatrice has a dental appointment, and I will ask myself why I even bother. But on the night the kids will be amazing. And they will remember it for the rest of their lives. And their parents will burst with pride.

Children are natural actors; that's what *playing* is. But the desire to perform for an audience attracts a certain type of child. I call them *Chianti Facilitators* because they are the ones who give me a reason to drink wine at the end of the day. I have a theory that their hunger to be on stage derives from a desperate need to feel loved and adored by those around them.

And nothing provides love and adoration more than a primary school show. No matter what happens on stage, by the end of the evening there won't be a dry eye in the house. Watching small children perform always makes adults cry. The combination of courage and vulnerability in the public spotlight always leaves grownups feeling choked up.

Then there is always that one special child who makes the hairs on the back of your neck stand up. Last year it was Keira. She played Juliet in our production of Romeo and Juliet. Never was a child actor more ardent in love; more overwhelmed by separation or more resolved in death.

There were enough tears to cause localised flooding that night. The parents cried for their own children while the staff cried for all the children. A few of us cried especially for Keira whose parents hadn't bothered to turn up.

Autumn is the cruellest term

13

Insect invasion

18th October 2013

Britain's unusually good summer has helped make our school's harvest festival a great success. The tables in the hall groan under the weight of ripe fruit, tumescent vegetables and freshly garnered tins of baked beans. But nature's abundance extends to fauna as well as flora, an example of which is currently spread-eagled against my classroom wall. It is in the corner above the sink. So far I'm the only one who has noticed it. I'd like to keep it that way but my chances are not great.

It arrived out of the green expanse that is our school playing field along with several thousand of its ilk. Alien invaders stimulated by unseasonal warmth and an instinct to procreate shrugged off their earthbound existence and took to the air. The chain link fence proved no barrier to an urge as old as life itself. Now they loiter against windows or hang like breath in doorways; each hoping to die with a smile on its mouth parts.

Things might not have been so bad if our school wasn't already suffering from collective entomophobia. My painful ordeal with a wasp during the first week of term has been blamed for this. Melissa still hasn't got over my pitiful screams and produces some of her own every time anything flutters within a ten-metre radius of her head. It was this that prompted our latest crisis.

The first twelve minutes of my playground duty had been only moderately eventful. Ryan was having time out for stamping on Nathan's milk carton; three footballers had been red carded for violent conduct and I had unilaterally declared the monkey bars a no-go area. I was just three minutes away from blowing the whistle when it happened.

The girls arrived with a sense of purpose that left me in no doubt that there was going to be trouble. 'A giant mosquito tried to bite me in the toilets,' sobbed Melissa. She sucked deeply on her asthma spray while her friends explained how it had, *'crept up on her … attacked her … flew into her face …'*

Melissa demanded we report it immediately to the head so the school could be closed for health and safety reasons. After all, the creature could easily suck someone's blood and give them malaria from which they would die in agony over several feverish days. She swore this had happened to somebody in her hotel in Benidorm. From small rumours great misunderstandings grow so I sent Ms Braveheart to investigate.

Fearlessly she entered the girls' toilets. Incredibly she returned alive. 'It's a daddy longlegs,' she declared. And as though her words were a signal to its brothers in arms others began to arrive in huge numbers, infiltrating classrooms and causing wild hysteria. Children capable of facing down plagues of virtual killer zombies in their own bedrooms became inexplicably terrorised by a few harmless insects.

'They're called crane flies,' I tell my children. 'They don't bite people, they don't suck their blood and they don't inflict deadly diseases, okay?'

'Why did one attack me then?' says Melissa.

'It probably bumped into you by accident,' I say. 'They're not very good at flying. They only grow wings for the last few days of their lives so they can find a mate and reproduce.'

'Reproduce means sex,' says Bethany, knowingly.

'Daddy longlegs have sex?' gasps Melissa.

'All creatures have sex, don't they, Mr Eddison?' says Bethany.

'Oh look, there's one in the corner above the sink,' I say, because frankly I'd rather deal with mass panic than explain the mating habits of crane flies.

Autumn is the cruellest term

14

To eat my cheese sandwich, all I want is

13th November 2015

To prevent the playground becoming a war zone lunchtimes have been shortened. They are now measured in nanoseconds, most of which I've used up hunting down the box of caps (flat and mop) I need to re-enact life in a Victorian classroom. Now the infinitely small moment in time I have left to eat my cheese and pickle sandwich is being threatened by accessibility issues.

A long time ago in a galaxy far, far away from reality someone decided to make our staffroom less vulnerable to wandering children and assertive parents. 'Inclusivity is a fine thing,' they said, 'but we live in a litigious age where careless talk can cost careers. Everyone knows that Mrs Acerbic's threat to bludgeon Damian to death with his own lightsaber was nothing more than an instinctive response to one Jedi attack too many, but you can't be too careful.'

Our staffroom door now opens only when you key in the secret code. And because it is a mathematical truth that in the digital age there are more access codes than there are atoms in the universe, I've been forced to write all my school ones (computer log in, class register log in, library access pin, photocopier account number, school email password and our new staffroom door code) in the back of my diary.

Because my diary currently resides at the other side of the staffroom door I mouth through the window for someone to let me in, but today is Friday and my colleagues (filled with the joys of the impending weekend) are being deliberately unhelpful. They reply to my increasingly desperate gesticulations with annoyingly flippant ones.

As a failsafe for those of us with malfunctioning memory systems and slow processing speeds, someone in the school security service decided that the secret code would coincide with a highly significant historical date. The problem is I can't remember which one. In chronological order I try Magna Carta, The Great Plague, The Fire of London, England's World Cup triumph, the First Moon Landing...

Just as I run out of ideas one of our young teachers takes pity on me. Unfortunately she is intercepted half way to the door by a dark and brooding presence. Mrs Rottweiler is neither young nor susceptible to pity. She also has several old scores to settle. As the last of my lunchtime disappears in the time it takes light to travel 29.98 centimetres I become aware of the irony of my situation. I am condemned to starve to death in true Victorian fashion by the digital indifference of the age of technology.

Then just when all hope disappears I hear the distinctive hum of a plasma-energy sword proceeding along the corridor. It rises in pitch several times before crackling as it makes contact with the imaginary weapon of an imaginary Sith Warrior. 'Have you forgotten the top-secret code to get into the staffroom, Mr Eddison?' says Damian. I nod weakly and he whispers, 'It's one, zero, six, six.'

'Of course, the Battle of Hastings,' I reply. 'Thanks, Damian. By the way, may I borrow your lightsaber for a moment?'

Autumn is the cruellest term

15

I'm not crying, there's just an old story in my eye

24th November 2017

To make efficiency savings in the education sausage factory, story time is being squeezed from the school day. It is being replaced by convenience texts and narratives reduced to their constituent parts. Classic tales are served up in bite-sized bits that have been dried out, reconstituted and served snack-pot style in order to aid digestion. But what's easy to swallow isn't necessarily nourishing.

Here in the twilight of my career, I will make a last-ditch attempt to keep great children's stories alive. I will make a stand against literature-by-numbers and low attention thresholds by reading Charlotte's Web from start to finish. Over the years I have developed unique voices for all the characters that never fail to keep children engaged.

Wilbur is a slightly excitable Welshman, Zuckerman has an unmistakable Barnsley twang and Templeton is pure Cockney geezer.

The only problem is that right now I don't know where my personal copy has disappeared to. I suspect Miss Bright of using excerpts from it to teach anthropomorphism to her six year olds, but I have no proof of this. And Ms Lemon is adamant that her papier mache construction of the solar system is made entirely of pages from the Sheffield Star. I scour the library but to no avail. There is only one place left for me to look.

I believe that if Charlotte A. Cavatica was still alive today, the cupboard where the dead books live would be an ideal place for her to take up residence. It is dark, mysterious and full of cobwebs. But most important of all, it contains an almost infinite number of Awesome, Amazing and Astounding Adjectives that would be ideal for use in her peculiar form of web design.

Helped by two small children (let's call them Fern and Avery) I eventually unearth an ancient copy of E. B. White's classic tale. Its cover is partially missing but its yellowing pages appear to be intact. Avery flicks through them to check and suffers a bout of coughing that leaves tears streaming down his cheeks. I hope it doesn't turn into a full-blown asthma attack, because I never wrote a risk assessment or asked him to bring his inhaler with him.

'I'm allergic to dust,' gasps Avery. He sips water while Fern tells us that, according to her dad, dust is human skin that is dead, and that if Avery is allergic to dust he must also be allergic to dead humans. I explain that dust is also composed of other things, including microscopic bits of paper. It is more likely that the dust Avery breathed in was mostly tiny fragments of old books.

I have almost forgotten about Avery's coughing fit when we reach the point in the story where Charlotte dies. It is a poignant moment and even now, more than thirty years since I first read it, I still get a little choked up. I stop reading in order to gather myself and to clear my throat, but just in case any child is worried their teacher might be crying, Avery reassures them. 'It's the dust,' he says. 'He's allergic to old stories.'

Autumn is the cruellest term

16

How to survive a one-boy category-five hurricane

10th November 2017

Getting a good night's sleep is not always easy. For three consecutive nights I've been awake into the early hours chasing problems round my head. They were only minor problems, but being slipperier than small children, I had no hope of catching them. So, last night I went to the pub, and after three pints of Farmers Blonde and a bag of chips on the way home, I fell into a deep and dreamless sleep. This morning I am refreshed and ready to take on Dane.

Dane has a stormy relationship with school. Today he is a one-boy, category-five hurricane, hell-bent on leaving a trail of destruction in his wake. It all started before school began, with what seemed like no more than a minor flurry in the playground. But as the morning wore on, fed by the warm, moist air of the classroom (and Dane's refusal to stop kicking his water bottle around) it gathered momentum. It reached maximum destructive intensity half an hour before lunch.

Like the Great Storm of 1987, Hurricane Dane is more devastating than anyone expects. Displays are violently torn down; books are uprooted and flung to the far ends of the reading corner; pencil pots are toppled and the maths area is deluged by a torrent of translucent counters. It is only when Dane's anger finally blows itself out, and he settles down under a giant bean bag in the quiet corner that the clean-up operation can commence.

The children are especially enthusiastic about restoring their classroom to its former glory. I think this is because the task is presented as an alternative to *extending sentences by adding a relative clause*. The result is that in less than fifteen minutes, what was a sea of devastation is transformed once more into an orderly learning environment. As a reward I give out Dojo points and finish the morning by reading from Skellig, by David Almond.

The children have previously decided that the dilapidated old tramp, discovered in a dilapidated old garage, might actually be dilapidated old me. It's true that we share certain traits. He is a miserable old codger. He likes beer and takeaways. He constantly whinges on about his arthritis. I smile to think that the children can't have read this story, or even seen the film. They have no idea that this sad old man will be transformed into a magnificent figure of celestial proportions.

After a while we become aware of a strange noise coming from the quiet corner. 'It's Dane,' says Alicia. 'He's snoring.'

I put the book down and shush the giggles. I know that most nights, Dane doesn't sleep properly. Sometimes his older brother keeps him awake playing computer games into the early hours. Sometimes it's the raucous laughter from downstairs. Then there's the shouting, and the arguments and the fights.

I resume the story from the point where Michael's mother is telling him how some people believe shoulder blades mark the place where our wings were when we were angels. There is a quiet murmur of disbelief, but no more. Sometimes it's best to let sleeping Danes lie.

Autumn is the cruellest term

17

With social injustice rife in the playground…

14th September 2018

Nathan doesn't normally follow Corey's bad example. He doesn't throw a tantrum when his teacher suggests he might have made a spelling mistake. Or fly off the handle when his calculations don't add up. Or sit under a table and refuse to come out just because he's been asked to stop stabbing Maria in the leg with a pencil. To the best of my knowledge this is the first time he has ever run out of class.

Corey, on the other hand absconds on a regular basis. This is because, unlike Nathan, he is a free spirit. Traditional educational structures cannot contain him. Classroom walls do not a prison make, nor iron curricula a cage. So in order to circumvent his natural impulse towards unfettered liberty, Corey's teacher sometimes compromises and allows him to learn *outside* with the support of a supervising adult.

On Corey's livelier days (providing air temperature is above zero, rain is less than torrential and average wind speeds are below gale force eight) he makes use of our outdoor provision and can often be seen studying forces (kicking a ball against a wall), solving practical maths problems (calculating how many Lego bricks he can throw onto the roof) or developing his language skills (asking people to go away using a well-known phrasal verb beginning with f).

The only drawback to Corey learning al fresco is that he occasionally gives his supervising adult the slip. This mainly happens when his attention is allowed to wander, like today when it wandered in the direction of Nathan's E scooter. While Nathan was dutifully ordering decimal fractions from smallest to largest, Corey was accessing our inaccessible cycle storage unit and twocking Nathan's expensive new toy.

In Corey's world, twocking (taking someone else's vehicle without their consent) is not a crime. His free spirit refuses to recognise the concept of other people's property. In the words of John Lennon he imagines a world with no possessions. You may say he's a dreamer, but his philosophy is essentially one that believes in the common ownership of the means of propulsion.

Personally I blame austerity. Welfare cuts have widened the gulf between the haves and the have-nots. Social injustice in the playground is rife and Nathan's E scooter is not the only shiny example of affluence in the midst of poverty. The appearance of Marshall's power-assisted cycle, Katie's pink Segway and a rash of brightly coloured hoverboards has turned the place into a seed bed for revolutionary activists like Corey.

Seeing what was happening to his scooter affected Nathan deeply. He put his hand up but to no effect. He called out his teacher's name but was tactically ignored. As a last resort he got up and tugged at her elbow but was told to sit and wait patiently like everybody else. Before she could remind him that there was only *one* of her, he disappeared out of the door.

Watching Nathan sprint across the playground in pursuit of his scooter reminds me of a night in 1989 when someone twocked my Morris Marina. The only difference is he's not chasing after it in his underpants.

Autumn is the cruellest term

18

Hell hath no fury like a mum in a faux fur hood

9th December 2016

Bang-bang. It's cold outside but I'm *not* letting her in. She's early and I need to do my breathing exercises first. In through the nose then slowly out through the mouth … and repeat. *Bang-bang.* She can wait out there until my heart rate slows, and the frenzied clamour of the day gives way to calmness. I just need two minutes to find and release the inner airbag of tranquillity that will absorb all fear … *BANG! BANG! BANG!* On second thoughts I'll let her in early.

They say it's the size of the fight in the dog that counts. Tiffany's mum might be small but she embodies the predatory aggression of a pack of urban hyenas roaming a rundown shopping centre after dark. Everything about her is a threat. Her thin frame sheathed in a metallic-blue hooded coat with a faux fur trim is a threat. Her chapped hands and her pinched face studded with piercings are a threat. She wears the tattoos on her neck like old battle scars.

I flash her my most disarming smile. It's the one I used on Mrs Eddison after I forgot to mention that I was going to the *Steel City Beer and Cider Festival*. It didn't work then and it's not working now. The face glowering back at me reminds me of The Picture of Dorian Gray. I'm seeing Tiffany's future and it's showing significant signs of wear and tear.

Experience tells me that it's best to begin a difficult parent-teacher consultation by hiding some of the negatives under a carpet of positives. Tiffany is as bright as a star (and as remote and distant). She has intelligence (but not the emotional variety). Her workbooks show she is capable (of throwing them across the room). But our conversation doesn't get that far.

Mother, like daughter, shoots from the lip and comes out all guns blazing. Tiffany hasn't got behaviour problems. If she refuses to work then I'm to blame. If she's violent it's the other kids who wind her up. And everything else is the fault of this crap school and the crap teachers in it. And even when the storm blows itself out and she starts to cry, she continues to fight. Because fighting is what she does. Even when it's just fighting back tears.

It's embarrassing to watch a grown woman cry until you realise she's not a grown woman. She's just Tiffany sixteen years down the line. A lot more shit has happened in her life but the choices are the same. You either give in and go under or kick out at somebody. And if that somebody just happens to be a teacher, then so what? At least a teacher is unlikely to be drunk, or to return abuse with abuse, or to beat the crap out of you, or to piss off into the night.

Love in a cold climate can be fierce and comes armed with more in the way of teeth than tenderness. But then anger at least heats up the blood, and is a lot warmer on a cold winter evening than a thin metallic-blue hooded coat with a faux fur trim.

> Autumn is the cruellest term

19

Incy wincy spider meets a sticky end in my classroom

25th November 2016

There is a coldness at the heart of humanity. Dark days amplify our fear of outsiders. Those whose appearance and behaviour are alien to our own are perceived as a threat. Apprehension and loathing keep guard at the door. But is this desire to keep intruders at bay healthy? Is it right to subject those who exist at the shadowy margins of our cosy lives to cruelty when they inadvertently invade our space? Can prejudice ever be an excuse for cold-blooded murder?

Acts of extreme intolerance are often born of an irrational fear. Nobody expected him to be on the corridor in the middle of the afternoon. But other than being in the wrong place at the wrong time what harm was he doing? He wasn't running. He wasn't damaging displays. He wasn't stomping around burning with injustice, or kicking a football at Miss Watson's autumn leaf collage. Technically speaking he was doing handstands, but nothing worse.

Mrs Cunningham's screams gate-crash my classroom and I rush out to see what's happening. I half expect to find her being beaten to a bloody pulp by a child armed with an ADHD diagnosis and a unihoc stick. She isn't and I'm frankly disappointed. It has always been my view that any teacher worth their salt should, no matter what the provocation, resist the urge to shriek like a demented chimpanzee.

'What is it?' I ask.

'It's a massive spider,' she wails and points desperately at the floor.

I squint in the direction of her index finger. I put on my reading glasses and squint again. I elect not to mention my concerns about teachers who (encouraged by government writing targets) use adjectives to exaggerate rather than accurately describe nouns. The creature is considerably less massive than Mrs Cunningham's reaction to it.

Ever since I read Charlotte's Web I've had a soft spot for spiders. Normally I trap them in a glass to avoid leg damage. But right now there isn't a glass available so my only course of action is to encourage it to step into my hand. Unfortunately it misinterprets my intentions and having recourse to eight legs and lightning reflexes makes a successful bid to escape.

'Oh my God, where's it gone? I saw it scuttle across your shoe,' says Mrs Cunningham from her kneeling position on the autumn display table. 'It must be somewhere. It might be on you? It might have run up your trouser leg?' I sigh, assure her it hasn't, and go back into class. A few minutes later, Jason, who for the most part has an arachnid-like ability to remain completely motionless for hours on end, unexpectedly walks up to me and announces to everyone that that I have a spider on my sleeve.

There are three types of reaction to the news that a foreign invader has occupied a teacher's sleeve. One is to run away screaming hysterically. Another is to gather around it in morbid fascination. The third is brutal and simplistic. In less than the time it takes to say, 'Leave it alone, it's perfectly harmless,' Jason knocks it to the ground and stamps it into oblivion.

Autumn is the cruellest term

20

A child's shoelaces can tie your stomach in knots

23rd December 2016

In recent years new and exciting types of footwear have marched triumphantly onto children's Santa lists. Shoes are now being found inside stockings as well as outside of them. These include shoes with pneumatic soles, shoes with external springs attached and shoes that light up like Blackpool Illuminations. There are even shoes with hidden wheels that let kids bowl along pavements scattering slow-moving adults like ninepins.

However, looking towards next term and the more mundane world of new *school* shoes, it appears innovation has progressed at a more leisurely pace. The main trend here is one of gradually replacing old fashioned laces with Velcro straps. Colleagues hoping to nurse themselves through early onset exhaustion by swallowing large doses of alcohol might not want to hear this but it is a trend I would like to see continue.

I know the deliberate and persistent engagement and disengagement (particularly the disengagement) of thousands of tiny hooks and loops is painful to teachers. I've shushed my way through enough assemblies to write a thesis on *Velcro and the incidental abuse of primary practitioners*. But sitting in a hall that sounds like it's been invaded by a swarm of cicadas on a night out in Kavos is better than projectile vomiting your way through the Christmas break.

It is a little-known fact that children's lace up shoes are the single biggest cause of gastro-intestinal infections in primary teachers. While there is no scientific data to back up this view, the anecdotal evidence is irrefutable. For example, only recently I arrived home from school on the verge of a serious stomach upset after accidentally ingesting shoe-born toxins. It happened while I was carrying out playground duty on the infant yard.

The chronology of events was as follows. At approximately 2.00pm I was infection free. At 2.03pm I became aware of Brayden crying loudly and tugging at my sleeve. At 2.04pm I discovered Brayden had a soggy sock stuck to his foot and an equally soggy shoe in his right fist. Using only wailing noises and the word shoe (ironically pronounced chew) he communicated to me that I should help him get it back on. A task which first required me to untie his shoelace.

Between 2.05pm and 2.12pm I tried in vain to do this, but the lace had more knots in it than a queue at a chiropractor's after the Boxing Day sales, and it wasn't long before I'd used up all the resources at my disposal. My knowledge of knots faded away like a distant memory of scout camp. Arthritis protested at being asked to perform unrealistic feats of manipulation. My normally razor sharp analytical mind lost its edge.

By 2.13pm Brayden's desperate whines were calling for desperate measures, so in a moment of madness I quite literally got my teeth into the problem and thereby sealed a not-so-festive fate. With my contamination already assured I did not need Mrs Smug to come over and remind me that Brayden spends a lot of time in the boys' toilets. Or that the reason boys' shoes get soggy is because, like males generally, their aim is rarely as good as they think it is.

Autumn is the cruellest term

21

How do you solve a problem like Mary?

25th November 2016

"Casting the lead role in the nativity without leaving anyone in tears requires a Christmas miracle. Here, Steve Eddison, a veteran 'executive director of school productions', offers some divine inspiration"

It is the moment before the audience bursts into rapturous applause. The last strains of *Away in a Manger* drift into the darkness of a packed school hall and for a few seconds you can hear a pin drop. Well you could if it wasn't for rustling crisp bags, crying babies (not Jesus), and the quiet sobbing of the parents of the Marys. That's *Marys*. Plural.

I can't speak for God, but choosing one girl to be the mother of the saviour of the world isn't easy for a teacher tasked with being Executive Director of the School Nativity Play. As soon as the opening bars of *Oh Little Town of Bethlehem* ring through the corridors every wannabe star of stage and screen is pestering for the top job. Even worse, every pushy mother of every wannabe star of stage and screen is demanding to know when the casting of Mary will be announced.

In his heart of hearts the Director knows it should be Ellie. She's the obvious choice. She's meek, mild and modest. If he were God he would simply make an executive decision, send a couple of angelic messengers round to inform everybody of his choice and sort the paperwork out at someone else's convenience. But God is omnipotent, and has divine henchmen to carry out His bidding, and fears not the wrath of Anjelica or Anjelica's mum. If the most highly favoured Ellie is to get the starring role, the Executive Director will have to work in mysterious ways to make it happen.

How to cast a Nativity play
Cast the last first and the first last

It sounds counter intuitive, but the most effective way to cast a Nativity play is to assign roles in reverse order of importance. In other words start with the sheep and work your way up. For is it not written that *'the last will be first and the first last.'*

Minor roles

In the time it takes to say, *'Do not be afraid for I bring good news of great joy: you've all got a part in the Nativity play,'* the minor roles can be assigned and the recipients sent away to write their back stories. The timid flock together to hide behind a sheep mask and make baa-ing noises; the war-like march off to enlist in the Roman army; the virtuous ascend to the ranks of angels and anyone with a tea towel is a shepherd.

This leaves several girls all desperate to be Mary and one boy to play to Joseph. The next part of the casting process involves persuading the wannabe Marys that the part might not be all it's cracked up to be. To do this the Executive Director must play down the importance of the so-called starring role while simultaneously bigging up the main supporting roles.

Below is an illustration of how the casting process might proceed from this point.

Supporting roles

'Put your hands down, stop shouting *"Me, me, me,"* and think carefully about whether Mary really is the role for brilliant actors like you?' (A pregnant pause – no pun intended – may be left here for the girls to process this information.) 'I mean Mary is okay but it isn't a role that requires great drama skills ... No, Anjelica, she does *not* get to gob off at the innkeeper ... Neither does she get to scream and swear while going through labour without an epidural, Janine .... To be honest, Nigella, for most of the play she just gets to wear a big blue dress with a cushion stuffed up it ... That's right, Chanel, ladies never look their best just after they've given birth ... That's why I think you should first consider some of the other, more important characters.'

By now the wannabe Marys are wavering in their determination to play the part of the Blessed Virgin. While this is happening, the Executive Director must seize the opportunity to promote the supporting roles by stressing, in a targeted way, how each might be perfect for someone aspiring to be a star of stage and screen.

The Pub Landlady

And then the words of the Executive Director fell upon Janine's ear and her face did light up like a Christmas tree. 'Of course the innkeeper can be a girl, Janine. But she has to be a special girl. One who can look glamorous and wear big dangly earrings and say important lines like, "No room at the inn" and "Last orders at the bar" and "Get out of my pub!" in a loud, clear voice … Why don't I just pencil you in for now?'

Angel-in-Chief

'Obviously, Nigella, this stand out role positively screams for someone with a glowing personality and the ability to rise above the rest. Remember that her radiance and power must fill the heavens causing lesser mortals (boys wearing tea towels) to cower beneath her wing-ed awesomeness.' Nigella shakes her curls in the manner of one envisioning her ascendancy to greatness. 'And not only that but it's a speaking part too, for is she not the Herald who will proclaim the birth of the Messiah?'

Three Queens

Now the Executive Director turns to Dolce, Gabbana and Chanel, and inspired by the words of Mrs Eddison (*Wise Men is a contradiction in terms*) says unto them, 'Don't think of them as three kings but as three queens. Rich empresses who have travelled from the exotic east on camels … Actually, Dolce, the camel in biblical times was the equivalent of a stretch limo with tinted windows and a cocktail bar …

That's right, Gabbana, imagine yourself as a VIP, clothed in designer chic, dripping bling and bearing a gift the like of which you can only get from Harrods … It's like Waitrose, Chanel, only more posh.'

Herod

Here the Executive Director takes a deep breath, looks directly at Anjelica, and says, 'Now I'm looking for someone to play the real starring role.'

'Do you mean Mary?' asks Anjelica.

'I mean Herod,' the Director replies.

'He's a *boy*,' snaps Anjelica.

'*She*'s the ruler of Judea,' says the Director. And before Anjelica can protest further he reveals the ultimate truth. 'The best role in this drama, Anjelica, isn't some pathetic little meek and mild girl. It is a cold, calculating and bloody tyrant. A powerful queen, ruthless enough to order the deaths of hundreds of small boys. So what about it?'

Anjelica is tempted but not yet convinced. 'My mum says I should be Mary,' she argues. 'So does mine,' says Janine. 'And mine,' says Nigella. And suddenly all seems lost until, in a moment of divine inspiration…

Hello Mary Who?

And so it came to pass that in one last act of creative desperation all did become Mary. Janine, became Mary Mitchell, landlady of the Queen of Sheba. Nigella became the Archangel Mary Christmas. Dolce, Gabbana and Chanel became Mary Gold, Mary Frankincense and Mary Myrrh. And Anjelica became Herod the Great, known throughout the world as Bloody Mary.

And when all the other Marys had left the classroom, the Executive Director turned to Ellie, so meek and so mild, and said unto her, 'I've got just the part for you.'

Autumn is the cruellest term

22

On the 12th day of Christmas

19th December 2014

"...you'll need a little lie-down. The festive season is testing for everyone, but for primary teachers it's downright exhausting. Steve Eddison looks back on the seasonal whirlwind and gives thanks for having survived with sanity – if not dignity – intact"

It's six nights before Christmas and in this house not a teacher is stirring. A combination of cheap cocktails and several failed attempts to do the Lambada with Mrs Goodtime at the staff do have left me dead to the world. I could sleep right through to the New Year if several members of my family didn't intend to wake me at first light. They want me to join in the ritual abuse of a young pine tree sacrificed to the God of seasonal excess; to lay gifts beneath its foliage, hang baubles to its branches, and violate a fairy on its topmost sprig.

Breaking up for Christmas

The phrase sums things up for primary teachers. Having survived a term that lasted longer than the Holy Roman Empire and ended in a car crash of glitter, glue and tears we are presented with more of the same. It is like rewarding the heroes of the battle of Gallipoli with a trip to the Somme. Does the world not appreciate the Herculean effort it took to get this far? And of the twelve labours we undertook in order to survive *The Nightmare before Christmas?*

One word of warning

So hissed Mrs Wright (God rest her soul) while holding me pinned by the throat to the staffroom wall. 'We never mention the C word before December.' This was the moment when, as a new teacher, I learned that the mere mention of Christmas has a unique effect on small children. It is like giving them several bags of Haribo in a single intravenous dose. It over-stimulates them. They want to down tools immediately and get excited. They lose all sight of the fact that learning to be literate and numerate is why they come to school. For sanity's sake primary teachers must delay the onset of festivities as long as possible; at least until November is out. After that it's *Abandon all hope, ye who enter here.*

Two suitable parents

A modest and virtuous couple were Mary and Joseph; just the sort of people God needed to bring the baby Jesus into the world. Unfortunately the children most determined to get starring roles in a school nativity play are neither meek nor mild. My particular torment was how to persuade

Sharmayne and her mum that being a Wise *Person* is better than being the Mother of God.

'Think about it,' I whisper to avoid other parents overhearing. 'Mary was the poor wife of a simple carpenter; she travelled by donkey and gave birth in a stable of all places. Balthazar on the other hand was not only a scholar but a Kin…Queen who wore fine robes, expensive jewellery and travelled by the biblical equivalent of a Mercedes SLS.'

Casting the nativity play is a challenge that can only be survived when teachers are creative and fearless in selling the different roles. It is helpful to have a prepared bank of phrases such as 'What do you mean *only* a Shepherd?' And 'Britney may not have got a starring role but her doll will be the Son of God.'

Three core assessments

Was there ever a worse time to carry out end of term tests in reading, writing and maths? Just when the children are bouncing off the ceiling like a set of escaped helium balloons, the papers arrive. They land on your desk with the gravest of thumps. Suddenly it's like the end of the 'I love to laugh' scene in Mary Poppins. A distinct lack of enthusiasm combined with a deep sense of injustice descends upon the classroom.

But tests taken without enthusiasm are only part of the problem. The children's targets are based on last term's end of year assessments that – because of their key importance in a data-driven school inspection regime – were over optimistic. You can bewail the improbability of Daniel attaining level 2B, and bemoan the fact that you have neither the time nor the energy to complete all the marking, but it won't go away. My advice is to just get on with it.

Four tubs of glitter

When I was a child I thought like a child. And after watching the children's television programme, Blue Peter, I decided I could easily make a Christmas mobile out of wire coat hangers, several rolls of tinsel and some silver paint from my dad's garage. But it wasn't as easy as I thought and I ended up filled with disappointment, covered with paint and threatened with violence for turning my bedroom into a scene of devastation. Multiply that bedroom by thirty and you have my classroom in mid-December.

The dreaded truth is that Christmas creativity doesn't just consume valuable resources; it consumes the will to live. While there is some joy in the fact that you don't have much to mark; supervising the whole imaginative frenzy takes a huge physical and mental toll. And at the end of the day you have to clean up; and explain how PVA glue got into the carpet; and how it got into Megan's hair; and why she felt the need to cut it out with craft scissors. And finally there's the biggest question of all; how did all this glitter get into the marital bed?

Five riotous rehearsals

By Nativity rehearsal number five you begin to feel for Herod. I reckon getting Mary and Joseph to Bethlehem was easy compared to getting eight classes of over-excited children complete with props and costumes into the school hall. Peace on Earth gives way to enmity. Wise persons and shepherds confront each other, the angels are anything but angelic, the inn keeper is ready to bar anybody who so much as looks at him; and don't get me started on the livestock.

Like a Thomas the Tank Engine story every school Nativity play needs a Fat Controller. The problem with teachers is that they all think the fat controller (minus the adjective) should be them. So for every instruction there are at least three countermanding instructions. And it is a well-known fact that in the interests of festive chaos children love nothing more than playing teachers off against each other.

To prevent a slaughter of the not-so-innocents, teachers must decide who is responsible for what. For example at our school we appoint Miss Cyborg (ICT leader) to take charge of all logistical issues involving movements of students and timings of events. (She in turn puts this information on a spreadsheet on the school's intra-web-cloud-drive thingy that nobody over thirty five can access.) Miss Perfect is appointed director of communications and given first and final word on all operational matters. Mrs Himmler, for obvious reasons, is appointed behaviour supremo. The rest of us patrol the lines shushing, glaring and threatening.

Six bouts of bawling

In my experience if it doesn't include tears, fights, vomit and mass hysteria it's not a primary school Christmas party. The sense of anticipation built up over time leaves children barely able to contain themselves. When the big day arrives it's like taking the tops off several canisters of highly unstable explosive material and juggling them. The most innocent reference to Angelica's bright yellow party dress resembling a sick bag is like a spark to a flame. The most evenly administered game of musical knees can in a moment erupt into mass violence.

The Christmas party, like any potential conflict situation, needs buffer zones. To survive teachers must build into it moments that are the equivalent of a ceasefire. Dead fishes is always good for promoting a few minutes of profound silence amid the frenzy of battle. For a more sustained peace try a teacher-led speciality act. Telling festive jokes is always good, although I like to perform *The Great Eddisono's Amazing Feat of Mind Reading*. It involves six plates, a twenty pound note and nerves of steel.

Seven strains of streptococci

They strike when you most expect it. When the festive spirit has all but killed your own spirit; when your physical and mental defences are at their weakest and your joi de vivre is hanging by a thread. They are the killer throat viruses; the throbbing headaches; the flu-like symptoms that cruelly torment every joint and sinew.

It is a bitterly cold December morning but you drag yourself out to do playground duty. You sip a hot lemon remedy from your teacher safety cup and ask yourself why you didn't make that call in to the school office this morning. You could have spent the day wrapped in a duvet on the sofa, but you didn't. That's because primary teachers are not the sort of people who burden colleagues with extra children, additional tasks and the opportunity to talk about them behind their back.

Eight boys a sliding

The truth is boys up to the age of eleven have no idea that discos are for chatting girls up. They think they're for knocking them down. I know this because every primary school disco I have ever supervised involved boys sliding across the dance floor at high speed to create low friction pandemonium. The Christmas disco is in reality two hours of bedlam accompanied by flashing lights and thumping bass lines. And it can only be brought to some kind of order when you finally introduce that other kind of *slide*. I'm talking about the *Cha-cha Slide* by DJ Caspar. Leading children in this communal classic is the only way to get the majority of students in the same place doing the same thing at the same time. Obviously it might result in somebody filming you on an iPad and posting your moves on the school website, but then it is Christmas.

Nine babies crying

Performing the Nativity play is stressful. It's alright for professional theatres; they have tiered seating, online booking and professional door people. In our school hall, seating for anybody under five feet ten and not on the front row is restricted viewing only. Oversubscription is the norm and the only thing between Mrs Hope (front of house) and death by stampede when she opens the doors, is good fortune.

Then there is the task of keeping parents under control, which is difficult because you can't keep them in at playtime. Some of them might listen to reason but there is nothing you can do about those with crying babies. You can tut loudly; smile helpfully or whisper advisedly but parents with bawling infants will always resist any attempt to get them to leave the auditorium. The result is that when you reach the most moving moment in the play, the only infant not bawling will be the baby Jesus; and that's because somebody had the foresight to take his batteries out.

Ten pounds the budget

What seemed like a good idea at the time doesn't seem quite so good in the early hours of Friday morning. Not when you still have thirteen homemade crackers to assemble and fill with assorted chocolates. Obviously it's essential that primary teachers turn up on the last day of term with a small gift for every child in their class. But thirty times even a modest sum of money is a lot in the current economic climate. And if six years of austerity has taught us anything it is that spending money you don't have is not a good idea.

Thrifty primary teachers are left with no choice but to spend little in terms of money but lots in terms of time and effort. In my case this means buying two economy tubs of assorted chocolates for ten pounds, dividing them by thirty (eating the remainder) and making a personalised, chocolate-stuffed cracker for every child in class. A task that took until 03.00 am. Crackers indeed.

Eleven ways to keep children occupied
Remember the pitiful sight of Jim Peters stumbling around the track at the end of the 1954 Empire Games Marathon in Vancouver before collapsing only yards from victory?

Primary teachers do not be deluded. Do not let the last day of term lull you into a false sense of having made it to the finish line. Looking after thirty children while you dismantle displays, fill waste sacks and pack away resources is only several teetering steps away from disaster. Trying to establish a sense of New Year sobriety and minimalist good order in a classroom that looks like a post-apocalyptic vision of Santa's Grotto is a gruelling ordeal that should not be underestimated.

The only way to survive the horrors of the last day is to keep children occupied in ways that don't occupy you. Let them bring toys, play games, watch DVDs, listen to

Christmas songs and colour in festive pictures. In fact, without compromising safeguarding, let them do anything that doesn't sap your last ounce of energy. You will need that for tonight.

Twelve fancy cocktails
The staff Christmas night out should be treated with caution. The euphoria felt by survivors of the Nightmare before Christmas is a trap. Teachers, like people who have been held hostage or endured torture, can succumb to post-traumatic hypomania. So when you arrive at Club De Cuba and those Latin American rhythms kick in and the rum starts to flow, try not to be tempted by those two-for-one cocktail deals. Weeping over colleagues and making outrageous comments about senior staff can be embarrassing. Waking up the next morning and vaguely recalling doing the Lambada with Mrs Goodtime, with your shirt open to the waist and a pair of antlers attached to your groin, will only make the nightmare worse.

The Morning After
'How can it be daylight already?' I cry. 'Why are you pulling at my bedclothes? Why can't I be left to die in my own good time?'

'Get out of bed,' says my wife. 'There's a tree to put up, shopping to do, presents to wrap and… What's wrong with you?'

'I can't do Christmas this year,' I croak. 'I'm not well. I think I've got tinselitis.'

Part Two

Midwinter spring is its own term

1

Cold comfort

23rd January 2015

I emerge from a black sleep of death into the harsh world of pain and suffering. The room slips in and out of focus. I moan pitifully as someone approaches. She is wearing a bio-hazard suit. The worst thoughts flash through my mind. Do I have the Ebola virus? Have I contracted SARS? What if it's Bird Flu H5N1?

She observes me through a protective visor. The absence of a reassuring smile makes me think she is a member of the medical profession. I have a feeling that to this person I am nothing more than a combination of suspicious symptoms. She is holding something in her hands which she extends towards me.

'I've brought you a cup of tea and two paracetamol tablets,' says my wife. What was a visor becomes a pair of glasses. What was a bio-hazard suit turns into cagoule. What was a scientifically dispassionate stare morphs into a look of *restrained sympathy*? 'I'm off to Sainsbury's,' she says. 'If you think of anything else you need for your *cold* you'll have to ring me.'

Her emphasis on the word *'cold'* makes my illness sound like a minor one. Is my own wife without respect for the valiant way I have continued to provide education in the face of winter viruses? My sacrifice might be insignificant when compared to those brave souls engaged in the battle against Ebola, but in the equally infectious, if less life-threatening, world of the primary classroom teaching can also be an act of heroism.

Those who do not work on the frontline of the war against underachievement have little concept of the conditions under which primary teachers must operate. But then when were *they* ever surrounded by legions of moist students dribbling snot and saliva? When did hordes of small children cough directly into *their* faces? Or contaminate *their* every learning resource with several billion unfriendly bacteria?

Armed with little more than a box of tissues and a bottle of antibacterial handwash, primary practitioners must overwinter in some of the most infectious places on earth. But is it really necessary to put our health and physical well-being at risk? In the modern age shouldn't educating the nation's children be less like germ warfare? Shouldn't pupil-borne teacher infections be a thing of the past?

Through the fog of illness an alternative future emerges. It is one where all primary schools are marked out as being biologically hazardous. Teachers are routinely issued with protective garments before entering their classrooms. They are sprayed with a powerful germicide at the end of each day and all contaminated clothing is incinerated. Not a single microbe is allowed to penetrate their armoury.

Then in a more lucid moment I realise that none of this will happen. In this age of austerity no government will commit scare resources to protect the health of teachers. Our only hope is to take matters into our own hands. My wife answers her phone. 'Hello dear, are you still in Sainsbury's?' I croak. 'Could you get me some sore throat sweets, a bottle of medicinal whiskey and a bio-hazard suit, please?'

Midwinter spring is its own term

2

A lost cause

26th March 2015

'It's navy blue with a yellow pompom and ear flaps to stop him getting earache,' says Hayden's mum. We are in the cloakroom area investigating the whereabouts of her Little Angel's woolly hat. This is not the first item from Hayden's extensive wardrobe of winter clothing to go missing. Two more woolly hats, several scarves, umpteen gloves and a green welly have similarly disappeared under mysterious circumstances.

I can tell by her tone that Hayden's mum suspects me of being complicit in the case of his lost belongings, but this is not true and the fact that he has misplaced two maths books and a number of class readers since the beginning of January supports the view that Hayden is easily distracted and frequently puts things in the wrong place. 'Do you remember the time he got a piece of wax crayon stuck up his nose?' I ask.

Hayden's mum looks long and hard at her Little Angel. When she turns back to me there is just the trace of a tear in the corner of her eye. 'You don't think there might be something wrong with him?' she asks. I smile reassuringly and explain that it's normal for those of a creative and intelligent disposition to misplace things. 'I do it all the time; it doesn't mean there is anything wrong with the state of my mental health, now does it?'

She gives me a questioning look so I tell her the story of my missing diary. It is an item I have lost many times but have always recovered on account of it being fluorescent pink. On this occasion, however, it was nowhere to be found. Despite the offer of a substantial reward and several children spending their afternoon combing the school in search of it, its whereabouts remained a mystery.

At the end of the day all the likely suspects were gathered in the staffroom. 'I definitely had it in here at lunchtime,' I complained. 'The only way it can have disappeared is if someone picked it up; presumably by mistake.' I scoured their faces searching for signs of guilt but saw only sympathy and consolation.

Finally Miss Marple rose from her seat. 'Did you eat all your lunch?' she asked. 'And I don't just mean the sandwich and the chocolate biscuit; I mean your apple too?' I hesitated at the randomness of her question before shaking my head. It is a well-known fact that I rarely eat my apple. 'Then it is logical to assume that you returned said apple to the fridge. Ergo the case of the missing diary is solved,' said Miss Marple. She opened the fridge door and there it was underneath my lunchbox, partially concealed by a tub of low-fat spread.

Hayden's mum and I decide we should question her Little Angel further, but he appears to have misplaced himself. A brief search finds him back in the classroom proudly wearing his missing hat. 'It was in the paint cupboard,' he says.

I smile. 'Of course it was; where else would it be?'

<blockquote>Midwinter spring is its own term</blockquote>

3

It was the worst of times

10th February 2012

There was an empty seat on the coach that chugged away from a grey school building in a grim northern town. It was where, on a cruel winter's day, Little Mite would have sat had she not been sent to school so poorly attired. Her thin dress flapped forlornly like the remnants of summer shredded by north-easterlies; her winter coat looked as weatherproof as a tea bag; her bare feet, blue with cold, peeped out of her cheap plastic sandals.

Miss Cheeryheart wept. 'If only it were summer and we were going to spend a day in Scarborough, paddling in the sea. Why then my poor Little Mite could come with us.' But it wasn't and they weren't. And poor Little Mite had to stay behind and miss out on a valuable learning experience.

Miss Cheeryheart sighed at the injustice of it all before settling her charges into their seatbelts. The children were about to enjoy the historical benefits of a ruined monastery on the coldest day since Dickens decided to give Victorian social injustice a satirical kicking.

Meanwhile, in far off London Town, Messrs Cameron and Clegg dabbed their eyes with sodden kerchiefs in recognition of bleak times. Their determination that all should share in the costs (if not in the means) of repaying the largest budget deficit in history led them to speak most earnestly to the nation. 'These may be the worst of times,' they said, 'but they may yet prove to be the best of times for public philanthropy and the private sector will flourish like snowdrops once the tangled branches of an over-bureaucratic public sector have been allowed to wither and die.

'And there will be no going back on our commitments,' declared those guardians of public policy. 'For poverty must never be used as an excuse for failure…except of course where poverty of the national purse prohibits the implementing of manifesto pledges.'

History, who is the clerk of all things and keeper of the great ledger of mankind, will, in the fullness of time, record in red or in black the balance of this venture.

In the meantime, Miss Cheeryheart and her poor Little Mite had more immediate concerns, which were to avoid being crushed beneath history's juggernaut. For those appointed guardians of learning, even in these bleakest of times, had great expectations; in particular the expectation that sacred attainment targets must not be compromised.

To this end, they showed a Squeers-like resolve to extract the highest yield from the lowest investment by a determination to resort to using the biggest stick.

As the coach chugged northwards and as the empty seat beside her became more noticeable, Miss Cheeryheart began to weep. The truth slowly dawned on her. How will Little Mite's achievements look when she stands before the counters of beans referring to a ledger whose unforgiving pages have no mitigating columns against which one might offset a life lived in overcrowded and chaotic circumstances? Where alcohol and cigarettes take precedence over good food and warm clothes? Where 54-inch flat screens and knocked-off DVDs take the place of books and conversation. Where the only ghosts that haunt the night are those threatening violence. Where will Little Mite stand before a ledger unblemished by the evidence of a single seat on the great coach of life left unfilled because of one pair of cheap plastic shoes?

Midwinter spring is its own term

4

I'm off to an Arctic playing field...
I may be some time

11th March 2016

Neatly folded at the bottom of my underwear drawer are three thermal vests with matching long johns. They are made from a blend of cotton and polyester that has been double brushed for extra warmth. If Bruce Willis were to wear them, with bulges in all the right places and a few heroic bloodstains, they might even look sexy. I have it on good authority they don't look sexy on me.

Not that it matters because I bought them for functional not aesthetic reasons. A trip to Reykjavik last winter was not without its disappointments. A long drive through darkness and blizzards failed to reveal the atmospheric wonders of the Northern Lights, while a five-hour search for whales on a heaving North Atlantic came to naught but mal de mer.

On a more positive note, my underwear remained faithful unto the (not so) bitter end.

Of course personal insulation came at a price. My coat designed for polar explorers wasn't cheap. Neither were my double-lined corduroy trousers and merino wool base layers. To minimise the risk of frostbite I also acquired snow-proof hiking boots, a quilted woolly hat with ear flaps, waterproof gloves, a face mask to stop my nose freezing up and a flask for carrying emergency rations of whisky.

Given that I own enough cold weather gear to survive an expedition to the South Pole, it seems ridiculous that I should be freezing my extremities off at the furthest corner of our school playing field in a shirt and jacket. The bitter truth is I forgot today is the day we are saving the planet by planting a billion saplings.

Looking around it's clear I'm not the only one who isn't suitably adapted to being outdoors in late February. Several equally under-dressed children are trying to out-shiver me. The only difference is *their* suffering is a product of an interminable winter of austerity, whereas mine is down to forgetfulness.

'If we d-die of hypo-th-thermia at least we'll know we helped to make the world a better p-place to live,' I tell Angelica. But the notion of self-sacrifice is cold comfort to someone huddled inside a cheap pink bomber jacket. Her only desire is to stop planting stupid trees and go inside again. This sentiment is reinforced by an icy blast of wind that cuts like a knife and hurries me into a decision.

'M-much as I am enjoying p-playing my part in saving the planet we have a s-safe-guarding issue,' I explain to a colleague. 'S-some of the children (not to mention a member of staff) are in immediate d-danger of hypothermia.' After a brief negotiation my offer to take Angelica and half a dozen other inappropriately clad children back into school is accepted.

In class we pass the time waiting for our core body temperatures to normalise by watching an educational video. It shows how animals are adapted to life in the Polar Regions. The lesson is that only those creatures equipped for the harsh sub-zero temperatures of winter have any hope of surviving. The weak, the ill-adapted and the plain forgetful will simply perish.

> Midwinter spring is its own term

5

Once more unto The Deep, dear friends...

26th February 2016

Suddenly from out of the deep a monster looms; a sleek, grey killing machine is heading straight towards us. I feel the boy grow tense. His grip on my hand tightens. 'Don't worry, Dylan,' I tell him, 'it can't hurt us ... *Dylan?*' In an instant his grip has gone and so has he. And for the umpteenth time I find myself searching for him in an ocean teaming with shoals of school children in various shades of uniform.

This morning I was enlisted in our Year One trip to The Deep; a huge, shark-shaped public aquarium overlooking the River Humber in the City of Hull. I have been given the task of looking after Dylan who requires one-to-one supervision because of his special needs. These officially include learning and behavioural difficulties. Unofficially they include unnaturally fast reflexes and selective deafness.

I have read the risk assessment several times and nowhere does it explain why the oldest and least mobile member of staff has been put in charge of the slipperiest and most agile child. When I finally spot him on the next floor up I am relieved to find the lurking Mrs Grimdale has him ensnared in one of her octopus-like arms.

'One of the sawfish in the viewing tunnel swam right up to the glass and he panicked,' I explain. 'He knows it can't get him but I think he was worried about it eating Dory.' Mrs Grimdale looks at me as though the rumours about me beginning to show signs of dementia are true. 'He thinks one of the Regal Tangs in the Lagoon of Light is Dory from Finding Nemo,' I explain. 'I had all on stopping him climbing into the tank to rescue her.'

We re-join our group and I spend the rest of the visit playing *Thwart Dylan's Escape Attempts*. It is an exhausting game, both physically and mentally, and I'm relieved when everyone is safely counted back onto the bus and we can begin our long journey west along the migratory route to Sheffield. Inside the warm belly of the vehicle the excitement of The Deep gradually begins to take its toll. One by one the children (and some adults) close their eyes and drift off to sleep; but not me or Dylan.

He may have special needs but sleep isn't one of them. I suggest playing dead fishes but it makes matters worse, and I have to reassure him several times that, despite what Courtney has told him, the sawfish will not use their long serrated beaks to cut Dory into little pieces and gobble her up. Neither will she be consumed by penguins, stung by stingrays, torn apart by sharks or devoured by a Spotted Wobbegong.

Later in the evening my wife arrives home and hauls me from the depths of slumber. There is disappointment in her voice. I think it's because I'm sprawled across the sofa like a shipwrecked mariner clutching desperately onto an empty beer bottle. She doesn't understand how wearying it is to navigate the treacherous waters of The Deep. She's no idea I've been to Hull and back.

Midwinter spring is its own term

6

'Fast Hands' Mozzy taught me a painful lesson

12th February 2016

This morning I am trying to comfort Rory. During playtime he was involved in a serious confrontation and is still burning with anger and aggression. I've been asked to help him come to terms with the physical and emotional injuries he sustained, and to try to persuade him not to lose his temper again.

But it's not an easy task. Rory has a careless attitude towards his temper which results in him losing it on a regular basis. Today it led to a fight with Jeremiah which he also lost. This is his third fight in a week and he's lost them all. His success ratio might improve if he didn't pick fights with children who are bigger than him. But then he is quite small for his age.

Those who quote Mark Twain (*'it's not the size of the dog in the fight, but the size of the fight in the dog'*) perpetuate a dangerous myth. The truth is *size matters*. Mr Kettle (one of my junior school teachers) used to say, 'You're a half-pint boy with a quart-sized gob, Eddison, and one day it's going to land you in trouble.' And he was right.

My first and last proper fist fight took place during the summer term of 1966, when I was twelve years old. A minor disagreement during a lunchtime kick-about ended with me arranging to do battle with Mozzy Morrell in the alleyway behind the school wall. A year earlier, when we were at junior school, this would have been an even contest. Unfortunately, during the intervening months, Mozzy grew into a tall and efficient killing machine, and I didn't.

Not surprisingly, the Brawl behind the Wall didn't go the distance. The chant of *fight, fight, fight,* had barely got going when a bewildering blur of fists brought proceedings to a swift and bloody conclusion. Any faint hopes I had of a career in the noble art of boxing died that day. But what would have happened if I'd been more like Rory? What if I'd had a high pain threshold and a reckless disregard for my teeth? Suppose, for some bizarre reason, I'd *enjoyed* getting thumped?

Like Captain Scott, Tim Henman and Eddie the Eagle, I might in time have become famous for being a valiant loser. Failing courageously is a great British tradition that throughout history has won the admiration of the general public. Mozzy Fast Hands Morrell may have knocked seven bells out of Eddie Half-pint Eddison, but I won the heart of the playground. I was the one displaying the bandages of bravery and the scars of sacrifice. It was me that went back to school wearing my black eye like a badge of honour.

As things turned out my glorious defeat proved to be a one off. Long before the cuts healed and the bruises faded I made the conscious decision to avoid ever again getting lippy with large aggressive people. I'm trying to persuade Rory to do the same but he's not listening to me. For some people pain is an addiction. They need it to affirm their existence.

                  Midwinter spring is its own term

7

Terrorists and terror tots

11th January 2013

Overdosing on old films during the festive break has not been a waste of time. There are serious lessons to be learned from watching Die Hard. For example, the reason John McClane ends up running around Nakatomi Plaza in his vest, trailing blood from his bare feet, is that he knows it is futile to negotiate with Hans Gruber and his bunch of ruthless terrorists.

Put simply there are some people you can't negotiate with and there are some situations when reasoned argument just does not work. At such times the only successful course of action is to strip down to your vest and kick ass.

To illustrate this point allow me to refer you to an incident that took place at *le chien et le canard* the other Sunday lunchtime. It involves a mummy, a daddy, a potato rosti and the child from hell.

Back in the old days when *le chien et le canard* was still the *Dog and Duck* it was not unusual to see somebody getting a good kicking. Usually the violence was partially obscured by a curtain of tobacco smoke and full race commentary from Uttoxeter. During the property boom of the noughties, however, the Dog reinvented itself. It became an upmarket pub and family-friendly restaurant offering fine dining at reasonable prices. So you can imagine my surprise when I discovered the kickings were still going on.

'Argyle, please don't do that to Mummy,' says Mummy.

Argyle responds by kicking her again and repeating his demands.

'Argyle, Mummy has asked you nicely to stop kicking her,' says Daddy. 'You know we can't have ice cream until after we've eaten dinner. Now why don't you try some rosti? You like rosti, don't you? Look, Argyle … yum yum …'

Argyle, recognising this as an attempt to deflect him from his goal-oriented persuasive strategy, throws the rosti out of the negotiating arena altogether. It lands on the carpet close to where we are sitting. While Daddy apologises and scoops bits of pan-fried grated potato into a serviette, Argyle repeats his demands and maintains his negotiating tactics.

I smile at the wife in a way that says, *thank God it's nothing to do with us,* but she smiles back in a way that says, *do you think we should interfere?* So I smile back more firmly in a way that says, *definitely not,* but she smiles back even *more* firmly in a way that insists, *we should offer them the benefit of our advice because after all I am a primary teacher.* And before I can smile back in a way that says, *don't even think about getting us involved,* we are.

'It's so difficult to manage the behaviour of young children these days, isn't it?' says the wife. 'You can't smack them anymore. In fact you can't even raise your voice. My husband knows exactly what it's like, he's a primary teacher.'

'Really?' says Daddy. 'How would you deal with this sort of thing?'

'I'd use the John McClane method,' I reply.

'What's that?' says Daddy.

'Refuse to negotiate,' I tell him. 'Negotiation doesn't work when the respective parties don't have equal bargaining power.'

'What do you mean?' says Daddy.

'As an adult you are able to justify your position intellectually using logic and reason. A small child can't do that. Small children are socially and linguistically immature. All they can do is cry, scream and kick Mummy on the shins.'

'So how do we stop him?' asks Mummy.

'Well you could try throwing him out of an upper-storey window and shouting *yippee kay-ay, mother kicker* as he plummets to his death.'

'Pardon?' says Daddy.

'He's joking,' says the wife. 'I think.'

Midwinter spring is its own term

8

When the hunger of the game outweighs everything else

29th January 2019

Childhood obesity? What childhood obesity? Kenzie weighs about as much as second-hand tea bag. His arms and legs are like strings with knots in them and I've seen more fat on an oven chip. If there is an epidemic of childhood obesity that will lead to a massive rise in the incidence of type two diabetes in years to come, Kenzie isn't the best example.

Right now I am sitting in the dining room waiting for him to be prised off the playground to have his lunch. While I'm here, I do my bit to get children to eat properly. This involves encouraging them to use cutlery, to close their mouths while chewing, and to not spit out the stuff that's got green stuff hidden in it. Despite my best efforts, food accumulates on and around the table until it becomes a health hazard.

Soon I have no choice but to go in search of antibacterial spray and a damp cloth. But in the three minutes I'm away (my journey involves stopping Kyle flicking pieces of carrot at Janine and washing strawberry yoghurt off Alistair's face and glasses) it seems Kenzie has raced in, had lunch and raced back out again.

This is especially annoying because today I am on *Kenzie watch*. We have concerns that he's underweight and my task is to monitor *what* he eats, *how much* he eats and *how long* he takes to eat it. The answer to the last question is three minutes. It seems I will have to go and track him down in order to fill in the rest of his chart.

Finding him is easy, but when I reach the footie area and shout his name, he's too busy racing around with the ball at his feet to bother listening. I decide against compromising my dignity by trying to catch him. For someone who might be malnourished, he's remarkably athletic. So much so that it occurs to me he might be the answer to our nation's childhood obesity concerns.

Kenzie's *hunger* to play the beautiful game far outweighs his *hunger* for food. This means he seldom has time to overeat. Of course, getting all children to want to play football more than they want to eat is unrealistic, but it is possible to get them to reduce their dietary intake by signing them up to my new scheme: The Kenzie School Meals Initiative.

Fast Food for Fitness will be its slogan, not because cheeseburger and chips will be on the menu, but because eating time will be severely restricted. Children will be given exactly three minutes (the time it takes Kenzie to eat that portion of his lunch that doesn't end up in the waste bin) to consume as much as possible. After that, everything left over will be automatically cleared away.

Before I can factor in the increased *learning time* benefits of this, my thoughts are interrupted by cries of dismay. Kenzie has kicked the ball into the car park and must wait for a passing adult to throw it back. Excellent, this might just give me time to complete his lunch chart.

Midwinter spring is its own term

9

Dogged with doubts over fencing our children in

6th April 2018

We have had a new fence installed in our back garden. It consists of seven 1.5m high panels that have been pressure treated against rot and fungal decay. Subject to a number of maintenance conditions it is guaranteed to last fifteen years. And because Mrs Eddison insisted on it being aesthetically pleasing it came with an elegant trellis, flowing lines and an eye-watering price tag.

But its primary function is not to enhance our garden, it is to prevent Scruffy running away to the big wide world beyond. He arrived at our house last spring, having come all the way from the mean streets of Cyprus via a dog rescue centre in Doncaster. It was a journey that appears to have inspired in him a wanderlust that our former, badly neglected, lattice fence could not contain.

Gardening is primarily Mrs Eddison's area of expertise. Thanks to her zealous application of weed and feed over several years, our grass is much greener than the man's next door. What attracts Scruffy to *his* garden is the absence of a gate at the end of it. Now, with his best means of escape cut off, his only option is to cock his leg against a rot-resistant cedar fence post in frustration.

But what Scruffy doesn't know is that our new fence is there for his own protection. He has no idea that the big wide world beyond is fraught with dangers. Men who come from out of town and steal small dogs to train their pit bulls to kill. Cuddles, the psychopathic bull-mastiff, who lives just across the road. The vicious pack of Airedales at 32. And scariest of all, the semi feral ginger moggy (aka Resident Evil), who resides where he damn well pleases.

Harrison has a lot in common with Scruffy. He is largely dishevelled. He comes to school against his will. He retains a desire to roam the big wide world beyond. And he has no sense of danger. He doesn't understand that our *anti-climb V mesh fencing system* is there because we love him. Like Scruffy, he inspects it for signs of weakness. To the best of my knowledge he has yet to urinate on it.

Since safeguarding became the number one school priority, new security systems have proliferated. Escape-proof fences, electronic gates, surveillance cameras and door-locks controlled by intercoms have been installed. But there are two sides to every barrier. Fencing children in may keep them safe, but doesn't it also make them prisoners? And isn't our obsession with *educational* barriers (policies aimed at sanitising school trips, insulating outdoor learning and restricting children to a straight and narrow curriculum) a reflection of our need to reduce risk to the point of tedium?

Last night Scruffy heard the call of the wild and woke us with a volley of frantic barks. From our bedroom window I caught a glimpse of Resident Evil, standing by our upturned wheelie bin with a chicken carcass in his mouth. He posed in the white glare of the security light long enough to make a point and then was gone. Over the fence and into the big wide world beyond.

>Midwinter spring is its own term

10

In the great ocean of life we are all at sea

25th March 2016

During February half term my wife and I lived the dream. We sailed around the Mediterranean on a cruise ship that, according to a fellow voyager from Bolton, was the biggest in the fleet. 'Oh aye, it's higher than a tower block and longer than three football pitches, is this,' he declared; which is all very impressive until you try to find your way back to your cabin.

Size isn't everything though (as I frequently tell my wife) and despite searching the internet for the best deal at the smallest price, the thing that finally clinched it for this one was the promotional video. What worn out teacher could resist the promise of lazy days on a sun bed? Evenings of relaxed over-indulgence? The lure of romantic destinations across a wide dark sea?

On our first full day out of port we took a turn around the open fourteenth deck and discovered that dreams don't always live up to expectations. A thousand miles south of Sheffield, February is still February and it paid to be well wrapped up against a spiteful wind. The sky above looked as grey as asphalt while the sea below was as tempestuous as a playground full of angry children. I admit it wasn't exactly what I had in mind but it still beat the hell out of doing SPAG (Spelling, Punctuation and Grammar).

Any teacher who has ever felt the urge to put the tiny tumults and relentless turbulence of a busy school-life into some sort of perspective should try being surrounded by a vast empty ocean. It's a humbling thought that for all of our technological achievements and ability to manage the challenges nature throws at us, we are still naught but a speck in the vastness of infinity.

Even on a ship the size of a small planet we could still feel the motion of the ocean beneath us. It was like tiptoeing over a sleeping giant who is restless and hungry, and who might at a whim rear up and destroy us. But giants exist only in fairy tales and it was nothing more dangerous than a squally shower that forced us to take cover. Back inside our floating city with its bars, shops, gym, pools, restaurants, theatre, casino and every facility imaginable it was easy to forget we were on the ocean at all.

Later that afternoon my wife went for a Salsa Experience with flexible Felipe. I declined on account of an innate inability to swivel my hips or perform pelvic thrusts. Instead I watched the BBC News Service in our luxury stateroom.

Wedged between stories about a possible Brexit and the systematic destruction of Syria, was a brief report on the latest migrant boat disaster.

In the early hours of the morning, somewhere just beyond the horizon perhaps, a flimsy craft packed to sinking point with human cargo no different from us, had fallen victim to this same unforgiving ocean. While my wife and I slept, twenty seven people including eleven children were lost feared drowned. Their dreams for a better life turning into the worst possible nightmare.

<blockquote>Midwinter spring is its own term</blockquote>

11

Try a little tenderness

20th February 2015

'It must be lovely teaching primary school children. They're so sweet at that age,' says Marie. My wife pats my back to stop me choking on my bruschetta aglio salmone. Marie is the wife of my old mate Chopper Woods. We played football for the same pub team back in the days when football boots, like Model T Fords, only came in black. We became 'friends' again via the miracle of facebook and thought it would be good to catch up over a meal at La Bella Nosha.

While Chopper refills our glasses with vino rosso I disabuse Marie of her fairy tale perception of primary school children by rolling up my trouser leg and exposing my right shin. 'Wow, nice bruise,' says Chopper. 'Courtesy of a burly centre half was it?'

Chopper is dismayed to discover that it was courtesy of Zoltan, who is not some oversized thug with a penchant for lunging two-footed tackles but a slightly built eight year old. 'It happened while I was trying to restrain him,' I explain.

This morning Zoltan came to school in one of his less accommodating moods. Rather than take his coat off to begin learning, he withdrew deep into its hood and passed the time by repeating my every word. In the forlorn hope that he would get bored of doing this I tried tactically ignoring him and encouraged the other students to do the same.

They say ignorance is bliss but it wasn't. Although in retrospect it was better than the attention Ryan gave him after he hit him on the head with a triangular prism. Ryan has a very low 'ignoring' threshold at the best of times, and being abused by an item of maths equipment turned out to be more than he could take. His retaliation was swift and decisive.

While Maisie went off to summon *behaviour support* I hugged Zoltan to my chest. This was primarily to stop him counter retaliating. I continued to hug him even when raw fury had subsided to a series of heavy sobs. I doubt hugs feature much in Zoltan's day to day experience of physical contact.

Chopper shakes his head and after pouring himself another large glass of vino rosso sets out his own philosophy for improving school discipline. This begins with the reintroduction of the cane and extends by way of amputation to the death penalty. I sigh wearily and explain that brutality is something that's already been tried with Zoltan and it doesn't work. The only thing that's not been tried is love and affection.

I empty the remaining vino rosso into my glass before acquainting Chopper with some facts about the physical and emotional consequences of child neglect and abuse. I end my testimony by reciting a saying frequently used in our school. 'If a child is giving *you* a bad day, it's because *theirs* is a lot worse.'

Chopper reflects on my words then says, 'You know what I think?'

'No, what do you think?' I ask, trying to keep the irritation out of my voice.

'I think we need another bottle of vino rosso.'

Midwinter spring is its own term

12

What's in a dame?

9th January 2015

Last night I wore bottle green ribbed tights under a brown cotton frock pulled in at the waist by a black leather belt. I checked myself out in the bedroom mirror from several angles. 'How do I look?' I asked my wife. 'Totally ridiculous,' she replied over the top of her book. I adjusted my tights to make them less wrinkly around the ankles. 'It looks better when I'm wearing a beard and brandishing my quarterstaff,' I said. 'Oh no it doesn't,' she replied.

Oh yes it's panto time again and this year I am playing Little John in a local production of Robin Hood. I am tasked with trying to rescue Maid Marian from the evil clutches of the Sheriff of Nottingham. My final scene involves pointing an oversized crossbow at His Evilness and delivering those immortal lines, 'I have large weapon and I'm not afraid to use it.'

My wife and I wonder why someone five feet two inches tall has been cast as someone who, according to legend, was a fierce, warrior-like giant over seven feet in height? If his name was originally meant to be ironic are we now being doubly ironic? Or are we in fact removing all traces of irony to avoid confusing an audience unused to such subtleties?

Until I was fifteen pantomimes were the only live theatre I ever saw. They took place in the church hall and starred the local vicar. A man of the cloth cavorting around the stage wearing a voluminous dress over an enormous false bosom was a source of inspiration to me in my youth and helped shape my future leisure activities.

I had to wait until I was fifteen for my first taste of *real theatre*. That's when our English teacher took us to see Macbeth. We read the script in class so I knew it was going to be short on laughs. But what really disappointed me was a lack of opportunities for audience participation. *'What do you mean we're not allowed to* boo *Lady Macbeth ... But Banquo's ghost* is *behind him ... All this throwing in of poison'd entrails is fine, Miss, but when are they going to throw* custard pies?'

Nurse Millie (retired male teacher and part-time pantomime dame) is breathless after being attacked by a pack of feral Wolf Cubs during our Saturday matinee. Her barbeque in the depths of Sherwood Forest goes disastrously wrong. Her stove malfunctions and launches several volleys of polystyrene burgers into the audience. Squirting it with fake mayonnaise does little to calm the situation.

And the mayhem doesn't end there. Backstage the Merry Men have two minutes to wrestle Nurse Millie out of a frock trimmed with dangly bangers and strategically placed baps, and lever her into one with a target for the archery contest. Sweat steams off her false boobs. Her boxer shorts sag under the weight of a microphone battery pack. She curses when Will Scarlett traps her hairy back in the zipper. She's ready with only seconds to spare. 'Thanks lads,' she whispers, fluttering her false eyelashes. 'How do I look?'

>Midwinter spring is its own term

13

Have I blinded the business manager? I spec so…

26th January 2018

At around 1.15pm today the engine of learning ground to an unexpected halt due to unforeseen circumstances. Although it is true to say that our learning journey has suffered delays in the past (such as when the wrong type of rain caused the roof to leak and turned valuable resources to papier mache, and when firemen evacuated us for the day to investigate that mysterious kitchen blaze that never happened) none has been as serious as this one.

To the casual observer our school might seem calm and efficient. The structures of our learning mission are well embedded and not easily disturbed. Teaching, planning and marking policies are in plentiful supply, staff directives are running at or above sustainable levels, training schedules, display guidelines, lesson observations, data deadlines and book scrutiny timetables have formed a long tailback along education's orbital motorway, and patiently wait their turn.

But a school's greatest assets are its human resources, and our most vital human resource has unexpectedly found herself disabled. I am not referring to our executive headteacher who is currently visiting remote parts of her empire, nor to our head of school who is locked in a crisis meeting about head lice. To be fair, we have more than enough deputy heads, assistant heads and designated leaders to keep us running in several different directions for years to come.

I am talking about our School Business Manager – aka Mrs Pinchpenny – without whose say-so neither the smallest easi-grip pencil holder nor the biggest seventy-four-seat luxury coach to Yorkshire Wildlife Park can be acquired. Every dri-wipe white board pen, every laminator pouch, every class pack of multi-coloured counters must be sanctioned by her. She is the arterial system through which the lifeblood of school supplies runs and without whom our academic heart will cease to beat.

Her ruthless determination to balance wanton demand and frugal supply was legendary until this afternoon, when our entire administrative function juddered to a halt. Mrs Pinchpenny's problems arose shortly after I left her office having filled in the necessary paperwork for taking a group of children off-site to run a drama workshop. Was it a coincidence that our school should immediately be plunged into organisational darkness? Could I in some way be responsible for clear-sighted fiscal management turning to blind confusion? It seems impossible and yet…

My drama group are about to warm up with the Penguin Song. Everyone is standing to penguin-like attention ready to begin. All except Bella, that is, who needs to ask me one more question before we start. This time it's not about penguins. 'Mr Eddison, why have you got two pairs of glasses?' I feel my chest area and sure enough, hooked over the neck of my sweatshirt by an arm each are two pairs of spectacles.

This is unusual but not unheard of and I explain that because I occasionally misplace reading glasses, I sometimes carry two pairs with me. Bella sighs the long weary sigh of someone with a history of tracking down my misplaced specs. 'I know that,' she says, 'but yours are mostly brown and those pink ones look like Mrs Pinchpenny's.'

Midwinter spring is its own term

14

Coming unstuck

20th March 2015

'This Sticker-thon is wearing me out,' says Mrs Frazzle. It is Friday lunchtime and she is slumped in a chair in the staffroom reflecting on our latest initiative to improve attitude and behaviour. It mainly involves giving out reward stickers like there's no tomorrow. One glance across the playground confirms how much effort has been put into it. Children as far as the eye can see are wearing them by the constellation.

Ryan, who is now the first child visible from outer space, has the most. His sweater is ablaze with positive images, shining stars and luminous sentiments. This is despite the fact that on Monday he expressed a profound disinclination to take any part whatsoever in a *stupid Sticker-thon*. How heart-warming it is to see him pushing small children out of the way in his efforts to attract the attention of lunchtime supervisors who are giving out shiny pencils to the *most-stickered students*.

There is clear evidence that this latest initiative has improved behaviour and attitude in the short term. But does educational quantitative easing (pumping vast amounts of new currency into a school's reward system) work in the long term? Are we not in danger of creating hyperinflation in the sticker market? And what if devaluation sets in and our entire behaviour strategy comes *unstuck*? How long will it be before I need a barrow load of Shiny Superstars just to get Ryan to underline his date and learning objective?

Back in the early sixties Sticker-thons didn't exist. The only classroom currency in those days was Miss Heaton's stars which she kept in a tobacco tin in her desk drawer (nobody knew where she kept her tobacco). Miss Heaton's stars were the lick and stick type and came in two varieties. There were the much coveted silver ones that were stuck on work deemed outstanding in terms of presentation, effort and overall quality. Then there were the gold ones, which were as precious as they were rare.

Miss Heaton's gold stars – like the lady herself – should be nothing more than a distant memory now. Their reality lost forever in the vast landfill that is everyday history. But at least one remains. In a tired old English Composition book in a cardboard box in our loft, one gold star still shines brightly.

It was young Eddison's reward for a story he wrote entitled *The Wind of Terror*. Based on his experience of the Great Sheffield Hurricane of 1962, it is – in Miss Heaton's words – *a splendid piece of descriptive writing*. Stormy adjectives buffet the terrified reader; adverbs tear relentlessly at trees; similes crash down on the page like chimney pots; while that prince of destruction – the mighty metaphor – opens his mouth and roars…

'I've got it!' Mrs Frazzle suddenly un-slumps herself. 'What we need are those machines they use in supermarkets for pricing things up.' She rises to her feet holding an imaginary sticker gun in front of her. 'Du-du-du,' she cries as she pretends to affix several rounds of imaginary smiley faces onto imaginary children. At least that's what I think she's doing.

Midwinter spring is its own term

15

Going viral

14th February 2014

William's face is the colour of left-over cauliflower cheese and he is complaining of stomach ache. 'I think he'd be better off at home,' I tell his mum.

'If he's not ill enough for the doctor to give him antibiotics he's not ill enough to have time off school,' says his mum. I have an idea she is unhappy about the outcome of a recent medical consultation.

'But has the doctor said it's alright for him to come to school?' I ask.

'It's just a twenty-four-hour bug that's going round,' she says. 'According to the doctor he doesn't even need antibiotics. That's according to the doctor.'

'I see but is he, *according to the doctor*, okay to come to school?' I persist. 'You see I'm worried about him infecting the other children.' Actually I'm worried about him infecting me but before I can persuade her to rethink her decision William's mother has left. I think she's on a mission to spread the word about the decline in General Practice.

It is a fact that the overuse of antibiotics has led to some strains of bacteria becoming resistant. Imagine your everyday antibiotic is a super-head sent in to turn around a school in difficulties. The first priority for him or her is to terrorise everybody – staff and children alike – in order to make sure the troublesome minority are well and truly zapped.

But troublesome minorities are good at surviving. And because what doesn't kill you makes you stronger they return at a later date more determined than ever to increase disorder and drag down standards. Now an even tougher super-head is required.

It's a bit like *clap a rhythm, blow a kiss, fold your arms and look this way.* At the beginning of the year this was how I got children to pay attention. 'I clap a rhythm and you clap it back; I blow a kiss and you blow it back; I fold my arms and look at you, you fold your arms and look at me, okay?'

It worked like a dream for three weeks. By week four a couple of children refused to clap. By week five the same children and one or two more stopped blowing kisses. By week six half a dozen children couldn't be arsed to even look at me.

Children are a lot like bacteria. They carry a biological threat and are quick to develop a resistance to the methods used to manage them. Stunning strategies to boost learning and promote exemplary behaviour flourish and die overnight. New ways have to be invented. Old ways have to be reinvented. The struggle continues on an almost daily basis.

My latest method for getting children to stop what they are doing and pay attention is to use my *awooga*. It is just one of the sounds on my hand-held sound effects machine. One *awooga* means stop what you are doing now, two means put down your pencil and fold your arms, three means look this way.

After a fortnight my *awooga* is still going strong. And the good thing is that when the novelty eventually wears off another twenty three amazing sound effects are available at the press of a button. These range from terrified screams to disgusting bodily functions like the one I can hear now.

What sounds like a cat coughing up fur balls turns out to be William. It is good to note a hint of colour has returned to his cheeks. Unfortunately his entire table is now covered with something that looks like left-over cauliflower cheese.

Midwinter spring is its own term

16

Forget your troubles, come on get happier...

17th February 2017

I'm feeling out of sorts and in need of someone to take pity on me, but Mrs Eddison is too busy. She stomped out of the door an hour ago to attend an early morning fee earners meeting at work. Every month, she and other senior employees are herded into a boardroom and subjected to a sustained barrage of coffee, Danish pastries and bollockings for not meeting targets.

My own misery is more ambiguous and can be traced to several negative health issues. My arthritic joints are unhappy with winter and have stiffened their resolve against it. I have a lingering cold that refuses to stop lingering and a persistent cough intent on depriving me (and Mrs Eddison) of sleep.

The psychological effects of all this have been made worse by some particularly challenging environmental factors.

We are in the process of having a new kitchen and it's taking longer than anticipated. A frenzy of destruction saw the old one disappear in hours, but the new one is still in boxes waiting for the plaster to dry. As a result we have no cooking facilities and no downstairs water supply. Washing pots by hand in the bathroom sink, while your entire living area disappears like Herculaneum under an accumulation of dust, is a depressing experience.

One way to escape it is to go to school, but when I step out of the front door I find my car windscreen is bearded with permafrost. I eventually clear it using a combination of cheap plastic scraper and vapour-clouded curses, but now I'm running late and the usual migratory routes are crawling slower than seems kinetically possible. I arrive at school with seconds to spare only to discover I left my joie de vivre at home under a dust sheet.

With only a thin smile covering my sombre disposition, I open the classroom door and face the frozen hordes. School playgrounds are not always happy places, and the long age of austerity isn't helping. Brydon creeps unwillingly into class like a shadow. The backpack of injustice weighs heavily on Declan's shoulders. Hostility snarls from Shania's lips. And just when I think the last of my spirits will sink without trace, Kyle arrives. Now is the winter of my discontent made glorious summer by his beaming smile.

Life's not easy for a boy who can't do the things boys like to do. Being unable to steal someone's woolly hat and have them chase after you is pretty annoying. Not having the capacity to kick a football onto the school roof, or to hang upside down from the monkey bars, or to escape lessons by climbing the perimeter fence, is enough to make any student feel downhearted.

But Kyle's having none of it. From his wheelchair he laughs in the face of cerebral palsy; giggles at the inconvenience of living with balance and coordination problems; chuckles at speech and language difficulties and beams at the trivial consequences of having poor eyesight and impaired hearing. By the time his mum manoeuvres him inside our classroom my sorts have returned, and my physical, seasonal and domestic frustrations have paled into self-indulgence.

Midwinter spring is its own term

17

Mitchell's left red-faced by his body of artwork

31st March 2017

It started with 'The Weeping Woman,' and ended with an entire class of eight and nine year olds laughing hysterically. Who would have thought Picasso's portrait of his mistress Dora Maar would inspire such radical creativity and artistic ingenuity in a boy like Mitchell? It's almost a pity to ask him to destroy the fruits of his genius, but unfortunately the world is not ready for it.

I suspect Mitchell's mum won't be either. 'What do you think she will say if she comes to pick you up from school and sees that?' I ask. His reply is a grin. At least I think it's a grin. It's hard to read someone's expression when they've painted their entire face red.

I send Mitchell to the washroom and threaten any residual laughter with a spelling test. Like Uncle Albert's tea party in Mary Poppins, everyone reluctantly descends back down to earth. Before we continue with our *portrait painting* I need a little chat about the rules. 'The first one is that we never paint our faces,' I say.

Before I get to rule two (we don't paint our friends' faces either) Kira has anticipated me and points out that the she had her face painted by a teacher at the school fair and on this basis would like to scrap her interpretation of Girl with a Pearl Earring on A3 cartridge paper in favour of a Butterfly with Spread Wings on Demi Goodwill. I have no choice but to nip this idea in its pupal stage. 'School paints are not the same as face paints,' I explain. '*Face* paints are scientifically developed to be used on human skin with minimal harmful side effects. *School* paints are designed to go on paper.'

The children take up their paintbrushes again and I wander around the room doing my best to curb art-surface innovation by actively praising traditional paint-on-paper modes of expression. 'Corey, that *Mona Lisa* has never looked so enigmatic ... Your *Berthe Morisot* could have been painted by Manet himself, Danielle ... Bailey, that interpretation of Da Vinci's *Man in Red Chalk* looks like...' I want to say *Mr Twit* but settle for, '... *a masterpiece.*'

Only Alisha (who has lost interest in Klimt's portrait of *Adele Bloch-Bauer)* is still pondering the subject of body art. 'Having tattoos is like being painted,' she says, and explains how her mum has loads of tattoos ... including Alisha's name in a heart shape ... and how they stick needles into your skin ... and how you can get blood poisoning from it

… and how you have to have injections if it gets infected, although on reflection she thinks that might have been when she had her belly button pierced.

Before Alisha can reveal any more detailed personal information about her mum, Mitchell returns and we stop to make a careful inspection of him. Though there are areas of ingrained red around his eyes, ears and hairline, he is mostly shades of pink. It is a theme that has now been extended to include his school shirt and is evocative of the time I washed a red sock with the whites.

Midwinter spring is its own term

18

Ask no questions and hear no lies about dinosaurs

3rd February 2017

Triton is sharp of mind, sharp of tongue and blunt when airing his opinions. So when Jake assures us that his dad *does* have a red Ferrari what does two hundred miles an hour, it's comes as no surprise to see Triton take issue with him and call him a *big fat liar*. Apparently he's been to Jake's house and his dad's car is a grey Vauxhall Astra Estate. Jake strongly disagrees with this, so in order to avoid a head on collision and road rage, I suspend the game and recap the rules.

We are playing *Truth or Lie*. It is based on the popular television panel show game, *Would I Lie To You*. In our version the children sit in a circle and take it in turns to tell the group an interesting fact about themselves. The group then have three minutes to work out whether it's the truth or a lie. It's best if I model the activity first, so I begin by saying, 'I once woke up a five year old to show me how to work a TV set.'

With the timer set, the children start to ask me questions. Giselle finds out that I was baby-sitting in someone else's house. Daniel establishes that there were three unfamiliar remote controls in the room. Zac recalls my lack of technical expertise vis-a-vis tablet computers and electronic registers. When the timer pings the children unanimously agree that I was telling the truth. And of course they are right, but in hindsight I should have started with a lie. Now *everyone* insists on telling a *truth*.

Some of these truths are well known and much publicised. 'It's true that my dad lives in Doncaster prison,' says Karl. 'It's true that I went to Disney World in Florida,' says Shantelle. 'It's true that my mum had a boob job for her birthday,' says Clarissa. Others are less well known and slightly disturbing. 'It's true that I've got a brother and two sisters that I've never seen,' says Janine. 'It's true my dad lets me play Black Ops on his Xbox,' says Neon. 'It's true my Uncle Jack killed himself,' says Marty.

But as the game goes on it gets more competitive. Suddenly every truth is more amazing (and less plausible) than the last one. 'It's true my dad is an astronaut,' says Jaime. 'It's true my cousin won X Factor,' says Belle. And just when the boundaries of Triton's credibility reach their absolute limit, Jake's dad screeches into the stadium of honesty in his Ferrari and shunts him over the edge.

'Before we carry on playing *Truth or Lie*,' I say to the children. 'I want to remind you all that *lying* is part of the game. It's *okay* to tell a *lie;* and it's *okay* to *admit* it's a lie.'

There is a pause while they process this new information. Then, because I forgot to mention it should be a *believable* lie, William tells us about the time he killed a Tyrannosaurus Rex with a lightsaber.

'This game is doing my head in,' says Triton.

'Me too,' I reply.

                      Midwinter spring is its own term

19

Fiery arguments fuelled by our dodgy heating

3rd March 2017

Teachers who can't stand the heat should get out of the classroom. Mind you, until five minutes ago everything was calm. No one was arguing, no threats were being made and nobody was sitting under a table refusing to come out. The day was slipping uneventfully to a conclusion, which is as much as a primary teacher covering a colleague's class can wish for. Then we entered that treacherous time zone between *tidying stuff away* and *going home* and things suddenly got heated.

It is ironic that the cause of several fiery confrontations can be indirectly attributed to our school heating arrangements. Our ultra-efficient, environmentally friendly, state-of-the-art, computer controlled, under-floor system has one distinct disadvantage. It is remotely operated by an alien life-form who is intent (for purposes of future colonisation) on testing human discomfort to the limit. His mantra is, *He who controls the thermostat controls the world.*

This morning the heating was set to ten below hypothermia. I entered the classroom like Captain Oates walking into a blizzard; prepared to sacrifice myself for the greater good of human learning. Three hours later everything had changed for the worse. Now it was like teaching in the Water Lily House in Kew gardens. Plants unable to survive outside of the Amazon rainforest flourished in a tropical classroom, steaming with damp children gathered in after a rainy playtime.

By mid-afternoon, heat and humidity levels were at maximum discomfort, prompting Jordan to announce that he was sweating like a pig. To illustrate this (and to prompt concerns about childhood obesity) he removed his jumper and shirt. By the time I persuaded him to put the latter garment back on, every surface had sprouted sweaters. And because uniforms are called uniforms for a reason, the difficulties associated with re-uniting grey jumpers and rightful owners at the end of a long day cannot be overestimated.

In some respects a hot classroom is not necessarily a bad thing. One positive is that it can make children feel less inclined to take advantage of having a cover teacher. But the line between heat-related lethargy and heat-inspired fractiousness is a fine one. By home time sweltering discomfort has given rise to disagreements over jumper ownership, some of which spontaneously combust into minor conflagrations. Using every firefighting skill known to teacher-kind I extinguish all but one.

Jordan and Jeremiah are determined to resolve their particular ownership dispute by tug-o-war. It is a process that is stretching my patience even more than the garment, but they won't have it any other way. My best efforts to establish a cooling off period (calm words and cold reason) have thus far been as effective as putting out a forest fire with a bottle of Evian and a damp tea towel.

I briefly consider fighting fire with fire and raising my voice in anger. But that would be like pouring oil onto the troubled chip pan of lost tempers. In the end I decide I have no choice but to let their argument burn itself out. There is no alternative. Well there is but I'm not sure it constitutes acceptable use of a school fire extinguisher.

Midwinter spring is its own term

20

When the promise of the school play is the perfect carrot

11th January 2019

Something wicked came our way. Dylan tried to blame Jaydon (who gets blamed for most things anyway) but Jaydon was immediately proved innocent. When the theft took place, he was being held at Ms Rottweiler's pleasure for blocking sinks with tissue paper and trying to flood the boys' toilets. By a process of elimination the only person in the classroom at the time of the theft was Dylan himself.

But why would *he* steal Anjelica's unicorn? If he was going to steal anything, why not Jamel's lightsaber (left unattended in his drawer) or Mitchell's boxing gloves (that were hanging on his peg)? It's unwise to attach gender-specific labels to children's toys, but the very idea of Dylan stealing a cuddly pink unicorn didn't ring true.

And it's not only a lack of motive that's a problem. If Dylan stole Anjelica's unicorn, where is it now? Why is it not in his possession? Why is it not in an obvious hiding place? Did it flap its little pink wings and fly away? Did it use magical powers to become invisible and disappear up its own mythology? 'I bet he nicked it and gave it to his girlfriend,' said Henry.

Though Ruby turned as red as her name and protested far too much, the pair might yet have got away with it had their pleas of innocence not been undone by Henry disappearing out of the room and returning seconds later with Ruby's rucksack. Before she could grab it from him he pulled out a pink unicorn identical to Anjelica's.

'That's mine!' screamed Ruby, as she dragged it from Henry's grasp and hugged it to her chest. Angry tears and intense declarations of honesty, made for a convincing performance. I half expected her to threaten to pluck its horn from its plastic head and dash its brains out on our display of igneous, sedimentary and metamorphic rocks, if she didn't swear she was telling the truth.

Even when Dylan (who doesn't possess Ruby's strength of character) admitted to having stolen it for her, she continued to deny guilt. With barely a flicker of hesitation, she nailed her courage to the sticking place and admitted that, on reflection, Anjelica's unicorn is identical to the one she has at home. Maybe Dylan thought it was hers and took it by mistake.

It is only January but my mind is already on our school summer production. This year the children will be performing an all-singing, all-dancing comedy version of Shakespeare's Macbeth. But Year Six timetables are already filled to overflowing with SATs practice sessions, and audition opportunities are going to be limited. Unless…

Fair is foul and foul is fair. Out of the fog of confusion, an idea takes shape. Anjelica has her unicorn back, apologies have been made and no real harm has been done. 'So today I'm going to ignore what you did and thank you for admitting the truth,' I tell Dylan and Ruby. 'Now promise you'll keep out of trouble and you might both get a part in our summer production.'

Midwinter spring is its own term

21

A bruising experience with the beautiful game

9th February 2018

'Some people believe football is a matter of life and death, I am very disappointed with that attitude. I can assure you it is much, much more important than that.' When the late Bill Shankly (ex-Liverpool manager) said these words he might easily have been inspired by watching something like this. It's Friday lunchtime and the second half of a closely fought match between rival Year Five teams is well underway. But what started as a friendly has turned into the mother of all cup finals.

For this particular group of children the beautiful game is always more important than life and death by column subtraction and in their view the most important thing about school is playing footie in *The Cage*. Surrounded by a high chain-link fence to prevent the innocent from getting maimed by one of Zoe Blaster's volleys, our sporting arena is not exactly Anfield. But it does overlook Bramall Lane (home of Sheffield United) which is a source of inspiration for many.

Today, the rivalry between two randomly picked teams is more fierce than usual. Emotions are running high, passions are at fever pitch and safeguarding is in danger of being compromised. It will only take one more disputed handball appeal, a desperate two-footed lunge or a mistimed tackle for the ball to be confiscated and the match to be abandoned. What this game needs is an authority figure. Someone firm, fair and respected for her knowledge and love of football.

Cometh the dinner hour, cometh the woman. Who else but Mrs Shearer would dare to step into this cauldron of sporting intensity? Who but she would volunteer to referee the un-referee-able? As a mark of respect for such a courageous gesture, both sets of players agree to her one condition. Her decisions (including whether the ball went inside the jumper goalpost, under the imaginary crossbar or over the invisible goal line) will be final.

With the score at seventeen – seventeen, time is running out and a draw looks inevitable. Then Daz's high ball over the top sees several players busting a gut to get there first. In anticipation of irresistible forwards meeting immovable defenders, Mrs Shearer sprints up field with a grace that belies her robust build. She body swerves around Lee, accelerates beyond Wayne, side steps Aleesha and goes sprawling in the penalty area.

Being generously committed up front, Mrs Shearer lands heavily and in a manner that ought to bring play to an immediate halt. But this is football (which is more important than the life or death of a teacher) and the game continues without a moment's pause. Zoe leaps over Mrs Shearer's prostrate form and with Ahmed and Leanne in hot pursuit prods the ball past the onrushing Gazza to score the winner.

By the time the celebrations have died down and the recriminations have expired, Mrs Shearer is back on her feet again and making her way into school. From her stumbling gait it's hard to tell whether she's mildly concussed or simply in pain. Turns out her injuries include a badly grazed cheek, a swollen right eye and severe bruising to her entire forward line.

Midwinter spring is its own term

22

Studying dinosaurs, I was made to feel like the fossil

14th April 2017

Three years ago, on my first visit to New York, I suffered a stiff neck and slight bruising. I wasn't mugged, I just spent too much time gazing upwards and bumping into people. Walking through Times Square was like experiencing the world from the perspective of an ant. Viewing the whole of humanity from the top of the Empire State Building only served to reinforce mankind's insignificance in the overall scheme of things.

The concept of scale is a difficult one to grasp, even for adults. It is especially difficult when you're only eight. That is why I have chosen to sit in the belly of a Tylosaurus with a small group of children. I am hoping that by spending time in its digestive tract they will get an idea of the size of one of the largest animals that ever lived.

Our journey into the creature's interior began in the Late Cretaceous period, which for the purpose of our role play is just after lunchtime on a Thursday afternoon. There we were happily row-row-rowing our boat gently through the Western Interior Seaway (in the middle of what is now North America) when something beneath the waters stirred.

We cling to the sides of our craft as it pitches and rocks. Ahead of us a huge swell rises into the air. When it falls away again we find ourselves staring into the face of a hideous sea monster. It lunges towards us, jaws open wide, and swallows us whole. At this point Mrs Beardsley throws a black drape over us and our fate is sealed. 'Stop giggling,' I hiss as we sit in the dark. 'Being eaten by a monster from the prehistoric deep is no laughing matter.'

The start of the lesson had been anything but amusing. Armed with nothing more than a metre stick, a fact-file and an artist's impression of a Tylosaurus, we tried to visualise how big the creature would have been. To this end we marked off fifteen metres for its length and chalked in an approximation of its outline on the playground. But as every detective knows, a chalk outline doesn't shock like the real thing. Even after I drew in long pointed teeth and vicious eyes the children remained unimpressed.

To appreciate the scale of something this big requires more than a measuring stick, it requires imagination. So using role play we turn two dimensions into four and instantly transport ourselves back eighty million years. Even children who have trouble with *half past, quarter past* and *quarter to* the hour can do time travel, and acting out being ingested by a hungry Tylosaurus is easy-peasy.

When you are trapped inside the belly of an ancient sea creature with a party of school children it is important to keep spirits up. We do this by singing *The Dinosaurs Song*. When Mrs Beardsley removes the drape I congratulate myself that all the children now have a better understanding of the Late Cretaceous and the monstrous creatures that inhabited it.

'Were you alive in dinosaur times?' asks Zayden, as we walk back to class.

'No, I wasn't born until the Late Palaeolithic,' I reply.

Midwinter spring is its own term

23

Spiced-up healthy food isn't so hot without a perk

24th April 2018

It is the Easter holidays and we are in sole charge of our baby granddaughter for a couple of hours. Her parents are recovering from post-natal trauma in a darkened diner that serves hand-crafted burgers. I have only just succeeded in singing her to sleep when Mrs Eddison (flicking through parenting magazines) is shocked to learn that one in five children in their last year of primary school are obese. Her tone suggests that I'm somehow to blame for this statistic.

Unable to bear the thought of having to sing another verse of *Hush Little Baby* I conduct my defence in whispers. *Don't you think we haven't fought to free children from junk food's totalitarian grip? ... Strived to stand up against the insidious power of sugar-reinforced snacks? ... Launched numerous initiatives aimed at discouraging nutritionally-dubious packed lunches in favour of a more balanced school meal?*

Having long since banned sweets and biscuits (outside of the staffroom) school lunch is the only practical weapon we have left to promote healthy eating. But persuading children to eat vegetables that are essentially green and meat that hasn't been processed is no easy task. Sliced pork loin with steamed broccoli will always lose out to cheeseburger and fries; even if we present it in a colourful box, call it a Merry Meal and include a free plastic toy.

Spice up your Life Thursday was one attempt to introduce menus with more pizazz. *Why not indulge your taste buds with our devilishly tasty Mexican Chilli Con Carne (made from red tractor accredited beef) served with wholegrain rice and iron-rich green beans? Or if you prefer a vegetarian option, then treat yourself to a deliciously fiery Mexican Bean Wrap instead?*

Unfortunately the response wasn't quite as spicy as the menu, although if my presentation idea had been met with more enthusiasm things might have worked out differently. The sight of the school cook wearing a traditional red dress and dancing a flamenco on the table while her staff strummed guitars, clacked castanets and shook their maracas, could only have improved the overall culinary experience.

When imaginative menus coupled with clever marketing ploys failed to improve the take up of school lunches, we decided to ask some hard questions about what motivates children (and adults) to defy serious health risks in order to pursue an unwholesome diet. Could it be something as simple as the desire to gamble? And if so, how could we use this impulse to encourage children to eat a school lunch?

During the week prior to the Easter break our *Great School Lunch Lottery* took place. The chance of finding a *Prize Sticker* on the bottom of a dinner plate was met with much enthusiasm. And despite a few minor disasters (prior to the children being warned that anybody else caught looking at the bottom of their plate before clearing it would be disqualified) the whole thing was a great success. Or it would have been but for some disquiet over the prizes.

'They won what?' cries Mrs Eddison, in a voice loud enough to wake a new granddaughter from a shallow sleep. 'Chocolate Easter eggs?'

Part Three

Summer term views

1

The curious incident of a murdered dog in playtime

17th June 2016

I am drawn to a playground kerfuffle like your average person is drawn to the dentist. Reluctantly. Gathering children like a trawler gathers seabirds I proceed towards the crisis zone. After forcing my way through ranks of onlookers I find Addison threatening to beat up anyone within beating-up distance. At my intervention he crumples into a heap of misery.

Because experience tells me the situation remains volatile I proceed with caution. There are two Addisons. The one that makes Oliver Twist look cared for and one that makes your average wasp look harmless. The urge to comfort and the urge to avoid a flailing boot circle each other warily until he stops issuing random death threats. When he's comparatively calm I enquire about the cause of his distress.

The reason he's upset is because during the previous evening his dog died. Never again will little Scruff (that's the dog not Addison) roam the estate happily soiling pavements. No more will he hump items of soft furnishing or passing strangers' legs. The days of licking Addison's face with a tongue that previously licked his own testicles are over.

I tell him all about the time our Rover got knocked down by a Morris Minor and died in my Mother's arms. 'There's nothing worse than the death of a favourite dog,' I say, but my empathy is wasted. It seems that Scruff was only Addison's *second* favourite dog. Fang (who terrorised our playground last September) is his favourite. His third favourite is Slavverer, his fourth favourite is Psycho and his all-time favourite is Rabid, who snuffled off this mortal coil several years previously.

A more detailed examination reveals that it is the brutal nature of Scruff's demise that has made Addison especially angry. 'He was murdered!' he snaps. My sense of shock eases a little when I learn that this heinous crime was committed by a vet. It seems Scruff had been suffering from a serious illness that, according to Addison, made his belly blow up and his breath stink like shit.

Dog lovers often forget that deep in the soul of their family pooch there lurks a wolf. A beast that longs to slip its chain and follow its ancient instincts. You can stroke it and care for it and treat it like man's best friend. But you'll never know when it might turn and bite your hand off. Teachers similarly forget how certain children will ever be wild at heart.

I ruffle Addison's hair and soothe him by telling him how Scruff was probably in a lot of pain, and that the vet did the kindest thing by putting him to sleep. But the violence of his reaction takes me by surprise. 'He didn't put him to sleep,' he snarls. 'He's not going to wake up, is he? He stuck a big needle in him to kill him. And that's murder!'

Thankfully Addison's angry outbursts in time turn to smiles. The next morning he bounds as happily as a Jack Russell chasing a stick across the playground. 'Guess what, Mr Eddison,' he yaps, jumping up and down in front of me. 'We've got a new dog, called Killer.'

Summer term views

2

A rash trick

11th April 2014

I fold my arms and wait for the hullaballoo to subside. The look of grave concern on my face is there to kill off giddiness. It has been a giddy sort of playtime and some of it has invited itself back into my classroom. And it's not difficult to *spot* the cause.

'That's a strange looking rash you've got there, William,' I say, once a degree of calm has been established. 'I think you had better let me take a closer look at it.' He comes out to the front wearing what appears to be a rare skin condition. He is also wearing the sort of grin that requires his teacher to take a deep breath and count to ten. I pick off sporadic bursts of giggling one by one with my steely gaze until William is the only one left smiling. *Well not for much longer, sunshine.*

With the aid of a magnifying glass I carry out a long and detailed examination of his rash. My conclusion is that the situation is much more serious than I first thought. By now William is not sure whether to grin or to look worried. He settles for appearing slightly confused in a highly colourful way.

My investigation reveals that his face and arms are covered with identical green spots vaguely reminiscent of trading stamps. If this was the Seventies I could swap him in for a lava lamp and an instamatic camera. Each spot is about a centimetre in diameter and bears the outline of something resembling a four-leaf clover. Amusingly he has one on the very tip of his nose. Curiously he has one in the centre of each lens of his glasses.

I replace the magnifying glass and ask him questions about the general state of his health. *'Do you have a headache, William? Is your throat sore? Are you suffering from stomach pains? What about pins and needles?'* When he answers *no* to each one I frown deeply and announce that his condition is more serious than I first thought.

After shushing those students who are desperate to help me diagnose the true nature of his condition, I go on to make a solemn announcement. 'I'm sorry, children, but I'm afraid it looks like William has contracted *Green Measles*. Unfortunately it is the worst kind of measles you can get. It's highly contagious and often fatal.'

Isabel asks me what *contagious* means and I explain that it means you can catch it very, very easily. Several children who have shuffled their chairs closer to the front so as not to miss anything begin to shuffle them back again.

'I know what *fatal* means,' says Ryan, 'it means you're going to die.' To exemplify this he makes a desperate choking noise. There is yet more shuffling of chairs.

'Don't worry, William,' I say. 'It's not fatal if you diagnose it early and get the right treatment. And as I distinctly remember you had no sign of Green Measles before playtime I think there is a good chance you can be saved. Now before I ask the office to ring the emergency services and an ambulance comes to rush you to hospital, can you think of any other reason why you might be covered in bright green spots?'

William examines his feet for several seconds before taking something out of his pocket. He hands it to me without looking up.

'What's this?' I ask.

'It's my grandma's lucky bingo dabber,' he says.

'Ah, William, you are a card,' I reply.

Summer term views

3

The answer isn't always to burst unscientific bubbles

11th April 2014

With varying degrees of reluctance the children get into their science discussion groups. Their first task is to come up with a possible answer to the question, *What are bubbles?* Each group has five minutes to agree an explanation, write it on a Post-it, and attach it to the whiteboard. Tensions amongst the Einsteins are such that I eventually give in and allow one of them to write her own.

Angelina refuses to budge in her belief that bubbles are tiny spaceships. Apparently they are the only things light enough to carry wishes to the secret place where dreams are made to come true. It's what her Nannan told her and all attempts to force her to adopt a more scientific explanation are met with uncompromising resistance. Her final words on the subject are, 'Well if bubbles don't contain wishes, why have they got rainbows in them?'

As chief spokesperson for the Einsteins, Benjamin treats Angelina's argument with the contempt he feels it deserves. Science is his favourite subject and he already knows that rainbows are caused by the refraction of light and that bubbles are pockets of air trapped inside a thin film of soap and water. He writes this information on a pink Post-it and attaches it emphatically to the whiteboard.

Our next task is to test three different soap solutions in order to determine which produces the best bubbles. To make it a fair test, we decide the thing we will *change* is the solution, the thing we will *keep the same* is the number of blows and the thing we will *measure* is how long the bubbles last for. Benjamin takes charge of the chart for recording his group's results, and appoints Charlize to operate the stopwatch and Joe to blow the bubbles.

After a heated discussion (and in the interests of harmony among the scientific community of Einsteins) Angelina is allowed to conduct her own investigation. That way Benjamin can't get bossy and pick on her and tell her what to do all the time. To avoid any obstacles and a confusion of bubbles, we carry out our tests on the playing field. Each group finds a space well away from all the others. Angelina is furthest away of all.

'Faster than light in a vacuum,' I joke, when Einsteins are the first to finish. According to Benjamin's record chart, Solution B (a proprietary brand of bubble making solution) is the clear winner. Solutions A (shampoo with added water and glycerine) and C (shampoo with added water only) are second and third respectively. These results are soon confirmed by Faradays, Newtons, Darwins and Curies. Now we are waiting for only one person.

With everyone lined up and waiting to go back into class, Angelina is still out on the playing field. In a bubble of her own, she watches cluster after cluster of glistening spaceships carry her wishes into the air where they spin, disperse and one by one burst into nothingness. And while the romantic in me can't help admiring her innocence and determination, the cynic in me keeps whispering, *in your dreams, Angelina. In your dreams.*

Summer term views

4

Don't panic

20th June 2014

I need to get to the staffroom sink to find a clean mug. The ones in my classroom have several days' worth of fungal growth inside. Unfortunately Miss Brighthope is barring the way. She is on her hands and knees carrying out a detailed inspection of the floor. Is she in crisis or has she lost a contact lens?

'It's a drugs problem,' explains Ms Fleming, without looking up from labelling airtight self-sealing food bags with a permanent marker.

It would be easy to assume the pressures of marking end of year assessments, writing reports and managing a class of stir-crazy eight-year-olds has got to Miss Brighthope, but they haven't. She dropped an extra-strong painkiller on the floor and can't find it. Now she's worrying about what might happen if a child were to pick it up.

We live in litigious times and current safeguarding regulations require us to take no chances.

The probability that an eagle-eyed child will wander unaccompanied into the staffroom, spot the offending capsule, mistake it for a sweet, swallow it, fall into a drug-induced coma and have to be rushed to hospital is remote. The consequences if it did happen, however, are horrific. When Miss Brighthope explains this, more members of staff than the floor area can reasonably sustain feel obliged to join in the fingertip search.

For reasons of old age, failing eyesight and a ham sandwich, I decline to participate. I do however offer advice such as … *Let's set up a pill finding working party … Why don't we cordon off the staffroom with hazard tape? … Good idea to pull the dishwasher out, it's the first place a child will look.*

How we intend to keep students safe figures prominently in our school development plan. Our children can now happily hang upside from the monkey bars in the sure and certain knowledge that should they fall their heads will bounce off the rubberised flooring. Visits to the local park are relaxed thanks to the reassurance of a six-page risk assessment. Conker players can slug it out unscathed thanks to safety goggles, hard hats and armour-plated gauntlets.

I suggest health and safety may have gone slightly batty, but Ms Fleming, who is in the middle of preparing for her children to carry out an investigation into the best conditions for growing mould on bread, disagrees. 'You can't be too careful,' she says. 'The planning guidelines for this experiment state that it's vitally important to keep the slices of bread in sealable, airtight food bags.'

'Why's that?' I ask.

'Because exposure to mould spores can seriously damage a child's health,' says Ms Fleming. 'Particularly if the child suffers from allergies or asthma. Did you know that some moulds, if ingested, can kill?'

There is a shout of joy. The missing painkiller is found. The risk of a child being rushed to hospital has been averted. 'Could you help us reconnect the dishwasher, Mr Eddison,' says Miss Brighthope.

I grab some of Ms Fleming's airtight food bags. 'I'd love to,' I reply, 'but first I have to resolve a life or death situation in my classroom.'

Summer term views

5

Storm clouds gather

11th July 2014

The sun is up, the sky is blue, there's not a cloud to spoil the view... and to be honest I don't mind doing playground duty on a day like this.

'What's that you're singing, Mr Eddison?' asks Bethany.

'It's called Raining in My Heart,' I reply. 'It was a big hit for the legendary Buddy Holly.'

She links her arm through mine. I suspect she may have ambitions to become a carer for the elderly and is using me to check whether she has a vocation for it. 'Who's Buddy Holly?' She asks.

'He was the Harry Styles of his day,' I tell her. 'But he died in a plane crash at the age of twenty two.' I look up into a clear blue sky where vapour trails gently dissipate. It is reassuring to know that disaster couldn't possibly strike on a day like this. 'Let's take a stroll around the playground and try not to spot any trouble,' I tell her.

It is unusually calm today. Perhaps the children are too hot to fight? I relax and smile the smug over-confident smile of a certain BBC weatherman prior to the great storm of 1987. I tell Bethany that my forecast for today's playtime is for it to be mainly trouble free with only a small chance of a light disagreement.

But the legendary unreliability of the British weather is nothing compared to the unreliability of a primary school playground. One moment Ryan is hanging peacefully upside down from the monkey bars; the next moment Nathan hits him full in the face with a water bomb. A major kerfuffle ensues. Children gather like storm clouds on the edge of a deep depression. Voices rumble like thunder. There is an imminent threat of lightning strikes.

Amazingly the fight is over as quickly as it started. In wrestling Nathan to the ground Ryan partially loses his trousers. His Sponge Bob boxer shorts cause squeals of amusement amongst the circle of innocent bystanders. By the time Bethany and I arrive on the scene both boys are laughing hysterically.

The heat is unrelenting. By mid-afternoon it's too hot to work and dark enough to need the lights on. It is a relief when a summer storm finally arrives. It begins with fat drops thudding onto the asphalt. Then the heavens open and all hell breaks loose. For a while the furious drumming of rain on our metal roof is quite scary.

So maybe this is a good time to tell them the story of St Swithin? 'He was the Bishop of Westminster and his dying wish was to be buried outdoors where the rain might fall on him. Many years later some monks decided his remains should be dug up and reburied *inside* the Cathedral. When they did this a violent thunderstorm took place. This gave birth to the proverb: *If it rains on St Swithin's Day it will continue to rain for the next forty days.*

'Is it St Swithin's Day today?' asks Bethany.

'Actually, today is St Ryan's Day,' I tell her. 'With a bit of luck the sun will be out again in no time at all.'

Summer term views

6

Picture the problem

12th July 2013

'I didn't know you were born in black and white times, Mr Eddison,' says Amy after we have established that the fat, blurry baby in the battered photograph is me aged four months. I am grinning (or it could be wind) out of a 1950s Silver Cross pram. The children think the pram looks more ridiculous than the baby until I point out that if it was still around today I could expect to get a small fortune for it on eBay. Ryan, who is always on the lookout for the chance to make several fast bucks, wants to know where it is now.

'Is it in a museum, Mr Eddison?' asks Amy, which is where I suspect the children think I should be.

'I doubt it,' I reply. 'The last time I saw those wheels they were an integral part of the best soapbox cart ever to write itself off on the big green lamp post at the bottom of Foundry Lane.'

Summer term views

'What's a soapbox cart?' asks Ryan. I sigh wearily and click the next slide up.

On screen now is a full-colour photograph of a beautiful baby girl. She has a familiar grin, no teeth and a big pink bow on the top of her bald head. 'Now who could this be?' I ask. Everybody points at Chloe but I am not convinced. 'Wait a minute, I know, it's you, isn't it Ryan?' I say and everyone falls about laughing.

The only child who hasn't brought in a baby photo is Regan. She says she will bring one in tomorrow only she won't because she doesn't have one. If there were any pictures taken in those first few months of her life they somehow got lost in transit. A lot of things can go missing on that short journey from birth to five. Especially when the route winds through various forms of neglect and several short-term foster carers.

In 1839 Robert Cornelius produced a daguerreotype of himself standing in the yard of the family lamp and chandelier business on Eighth Street Philadelphia. It is one of the earliest ever photographic portraits and it changed things forever. So astounded was the world by this development that cultures not grounded in a scientific method didn't trust it. Some believed the camera could steal the soul and hold it prisoner. The odd thing is they were right.

While flicking through old albums the other day I found a *me* I don't remember being. A child whose innocence contains the blueprint for all my deficiencies and a genetic code preset to deliver haemorrhoids and arthritis. Gathered around him are the architects of who he would become. Many are long since dead, smiling back at me from faces that look familiar and places I can only vaguely recall.

There is something reassuring about family albums. The fact they chart our existence from chubby-cheeked cherub to wrinkled old git gives us a unique sense of who we are and where we came from. It is vaguely magical to think that in this collection of old images I am bound to those that went before me and to those that came after.

Two days later Regan brings in her baby photograph and shows it round the class. 'Don't say anything but it's an old one of me,' whispers her adoptive mum. 'Do you think the children will be able to tell it's not her?'

'I doubt it,' I reply. 'They're more interested in the pram.' It's a circa 1982 Silver Cross and would probably fetch a small fortune on eBay.

Summer term views

7

The bald truth about our school's cue-ball kid

1st July 2016

Our new table lamp arrived in a box the size of a small car. On the outside red warnings reminded everyone that the contents were fragile. Little martini glasses indicated which way round it should go. Inside, as an added precaution, someone had wrapped half a kilometre of bubble wrap around a much smaller box that contained the actual lamp. This in turn was securely encased in blocks of moulded polystyrene.

If all fragile thing were handled with this level of extreme care the world would be a safer (if less environmentally friendly) place to live. But accidental damage happens, and the consequences are often serious. And because we can't put *children* in bubble wrap (the dangers of suffocation outweigh any safety benefits) teachers are often left picking up the pieces of broken ones and gluing them back together again.

Dayne is the latest victim of accidental damage. You could tell something was wrong when he arrived, on the warmest day of the year so far, with his head buried deep in the confines of his winter coat. His mum told us this was the only way he'd come to school. In class he still refuses to remove it and reveal the actual cause of his distress.

It's only in the quiet of the cloakroom, and after considerable coaxing, that Dayne allows his mum to peel his hood back and expose the awful truth. It is worse than any of us imagined. Gasps of disbelief are stifled and replaced by soothing words of encouragement as one by one we take in the awful reality of what has happened to him.

Dayne's happy, bouncing cascade of beautiful blonde curls is no more. In its place is a grotesquely pale, and extremely hairless skull. It blinks maliciously at us from out of the gloom. His mother explains that he spent the weekend with *That Waste of Space* (aka his dad) who convinced him to let him shave his head in some sort of father-son bonding ritual. Now they both resemble extras from The Boy in the Striped Pyjamas.

Because careless crops cost self-esteem there's no time to lose. A two-part rescue and recovery mission snaps into operation. Task one is to prevent further damage by warning of the dire consequences that will befall any child engaging in unkind laughter, pitiless pointing or making hurtful remarks. Task two is to put Dayne back together again and wrap him in several protective layers of positivity. These include telling him how grown up he looks, how cool he'll feel now summer has arrived, how he won't ever get head lice again and how nice his bristles feel.

By home time he's almost fully recovered from his close encounter with male grooming equipment. If anything he's enjoying the attention of those of us who can't stop stoking his head against the nap and sighing. Even his friends want to stroke him. All except Tyrone, who insists on calling him *cueball*. 'He's just jealous,' I whisper, and Dayne smiles at me. It's his old smile but, like most things that have been damaged and hastily repaired, it's not quite so perfect anymore.

Summer term views

8

Superheroes sweat but pupils merely 'aspire'

13th July 2018

When asked to explain what *aspiring* means, Logan looks confused. Mainly because when the term was being discussed by the rest of his class, he was busy trying to punch England captain Harry Kane in the ear using his extendable arm with a fist on the end. Apparently he's an *Incredible*, and one of his superpowers is elasticity. It's just a pity he doesn't have a super-memory because then he might recall what we talked about only ten seconds earlier.

We are having a *Future-self Day* and the children have come to school dressed up as how they see themselves in years to come. Logan's dream occupation involves saving the world from crime and injustice. To gain the required qualifications he is going to see *Incredibles 2* with his mum and dad over the summer holidays. Although he wasn't born when the original film came out, he claims to have seen it a hundred thousand million billion times, which I think might be *stretching* the truth a little.

What's perhaps more *incredible*, however, is the fact that Logan isn't the only child in his class hoping to pursue a career in protecting the world from evil through the use of superhuman powers. Tyrell is going to be Spiderman, Jermaine will be Captain America, Briony is destined to be Wonder Woman and Lamar will probably have someone's eye out if he doesn't stop twirling his lightsaber around.

In a world lurching in the direction of putting up barriers and encouraging intolerance, it's crazy to suppose you can have too many superheroes. But will we really need this many professional football stars? Can the future sustain an oversupply of dancers and singers? And what effect will a fairy tale princess, a vampire, a zombie and a graduate of Hogwarts School of Witchcraft and Wizardry have on the social, political and economic stability of tomorrow?

Not long ago these same children visited KidZania London (an interactive city run by kids) and know the sort of occupations a community needs to make it socially and economically viable. So where are the builders, engineers and plumbers? Where are the health care professionals, teachers and policemen? Where are the bus drivers, shop workers and people who help us claim compensation for accidents we don't remember having?

And even scarier than the prospect of a severe structural imbalance in the labour market is the number of children who haven't dressed up as anything at all. Are their futures already written off? Is it possible that by the age of nine some children are resigned to being tomorrow's unemployment statistics? Unceremoniously dumped on the scrapheap of surplus labour? Resigned to a life on a zero-hour contract of hopelessness?

Amid the gloom, Sam, stands out like a beacon of hope. He is wearing a suit and tie and carrying a calculator. He initially wanted to be a dentist but, as he didn't have a white coat, decided to come as an accountant instead. Before I can commend his flexibility and pragmatism, however, the *Incredible Logan* prods me with his extendable arm. 'I know what *aspiring* means!' he says. 'It's when you get sweaty.'

Summer term views

9

Best foot forward

19th April 2013

It's 04.00am on a Tuesday morning and I'm lying on the settee trying to watch a repeat of Fawlty Towers. My hope that a cocktail of co-codamol, ibuprofen and John Cleese will dull the pain is a forlorn one. The throbbing in my right ankle laughs in the face of extra-strong analgesics and classic comedy.

They said the first forty eight hours would be the worst, so only thirty six to go. By Wednesday afternoon I should be relatively pain free. That will give me nearly three weeks to complete a recuperation programme that involves doing bugger all.

It began last September when X rays revealed my painful limp was *footballer's ankle*. My mind went back to a cold January in 1984 when a particularly hefty challenge by the

Dog and Duck's right back brought my promising career in Sunday League football to a premature end. 'Isn't that what Wayne Rooney had?' I asked the consultant.

'He was an athlete with a broken metatarsal,' she replied. 'You're a tired old teacher with osteoarthritis.'

While we were waiting for my spinal block to take effect, the anaesthetist honed his skills by knocking out a fly in mid-flight with a freezing alcohol spray. 'Can't have the little sod getting into the operating theatre,' he laughed.

'Indeed not,' I replied, trying to dismiss a vision of writhing maggots and putrefaction erupting from my black and swollen ankle.

'As you can see I'm cutting away the calcified spur that appears to be causing the problem,' said the surgeon. By the miracle of modern anaesthesia I watched my operation on a fifty-two-inch flat-screen television. To my untutored eye it looked like some white stuff, some red stuff and some fibrous-looking grey stuff were being systematically chewed up by a thing with revolving metal teeth.

By Thursday the balance of agony and ecstasy has tilted in favour of the latter and I feel up to ringing my job share partner. She sounds fraught but does her best to be sympathetic. Then she reminds me that it's assessment week and my absence means she will have to do them all by herself.

'It's a pity I'm on crutches and can't drive,' I tell her. 'Otherwise I'd be up for a bit of marking.' I can hear the sound of squabbling children in the background and she has to ring off. I dunk another chocolate hobnob into my coffee and turn the sound up on Bargain Hunt.

By Saturday I am able to use paracetamol for pain relief. This is a medical decision and has nothing to do with the fact that you can't drink alcohol while taking co-codamol. I open my school emails and read everyone's heartfelt condolences. Some of them have postscripts requesting the whereabouts of resources I may have been the last one to use.

By Sunday afternoon, and with no need to make frenzied preparations for the week ahead, I am at my ecstatic peak. My only planning is for a fortnight of indolence: two weeks of crosswords, mindless TV, long afternoon snoozes…

My thoughts are interrupted by a firm rap on the door. I check my crutches are in a prominent position, adopt a supine position on the settee and elevate my heavily bandaged ankle. 'Come in,' I cry in a voice that epitomises stoicism in the face of relentless suffering.

Lara Croft (our hyperactive deputy head) cartwheels into the living room. 'I've brought you a little present from school,' she says.

'How kind of everyone to think of me at such a busy time, but they shouldn't have *bought* me anything,' I tell her.

'They didn't,' she says, and disappears again in a flurry of back flips.

I tear open the package to reveal a pile of unmarked assessments. Now where did I put those extra-strong painkillers?

Summer term views

10

Being an undertaker is the final nail in my coffin

3rd June 2016

Mrs Sorter solves problems. When a family is in crisis she is the one who will manage and resolve the situation. When new playground equipment is required it is generally Mrs Sorter who sources it, secures funding and makes all the necessary arrangements for its installation. Experience tells me there is nothing she can't acquire, sort out or fix. Even my unusual request for a child-sized coffin doesn't faze her.

Corpses come in various sizes so it's important we measure Logan carefully. His dimensions are one hundred and fifty four centimetres long by forty two centimetres wide. I relay this information to Mrs Sorter who relays it to her contact at our local secondary school who asks her to hold the line while she goes to find a tape measure. A few minutes later Mrs Sorter raises her thumb. 'It's ours for free so long as we go and fetch it,' she says.

Having been a primary teacher for over thirty years it's fair to say I have served the needs of the learning community with courage and dignity. I have abseiled off a building, had wet sponges hurled at me and stroked a tarantula. I have even paraded along Scarborough beach dressed as a pirate shouting, *'Thar be gold hidden in that thar sand.'* This is the first time I've marched down the corridors of a secondary school carrying a coffin.

It's a prop for our summer production but it looks realistic, which makes it all the more surprising that we attract so little interest. A boy outside his classroom fumes about injustice but pays us no attention. A girl holds a door open for us but declines to comment. A third child loitering between somewhere and somewhere else can barely be arsed to raise a disdainful eyebrow. As we pass through the busy foyer my humming of Chopin's *Funeral March* is met with indifference.

In the car park I cry in desperation, 'A hearse; a hearse! My kingdom for a hearse.' Not because it is the anniversary of Shakespeare's death, but because, after several infuriating attempts, I still can't find a way to get five and half feet of coffin plus two adults into one small hatchback. If Mrs Sorter would agree to travel *inside* the casket the problem would be solved, but unfortunately a fear of confined spaces gets in the way of her reputation and she refuses point blank.

Instead she leaves me reconfiguring the seating for the umpteenth time and goes off to commandeer a man who can. With the assistance of a passing caretaker we eventually tie the coffin to the roof. A piece of old carpeting is placed underneath to avoid damaging my car's paintwork. After several safety checks (and on the strict understanding we'll proceed slowly) we are allowed to go.

Our journey back takes us past a local authority care home that is under threat of closure. I imagine rheumy eyes behind net curtains peering out at us as we drive by at five miles an hour. 'I bet those poor sods are worried we're low-cost undertakers,' I say. Mrs Sorter doesn't reply. She's too busy thinking of a business plan.

Summer term views

11

To many people, Spag jargon is a load of bol

20th May 2016

One November morning during the Seventies my dad suffered a sudden release of adrenaline causing tachycardia, hyperventilation and dyspnoea leading to respiratory alkalosis. Fortunately nobody told him this and he put it down to a panic attack caused by having to drive to Great Auntie Hilda's funeral via the Gravelly Hill Interchange otherwise known as Spaghetti Junction.

Back then 'Spaghetti Junction' was a term that put the fear of God into older drivers like my dad. He had all on negotiating his Ford Anglia around the nation's B roads. Unravelling pasta-style motorway mergers was his worst nightmare. His was a world with no satellite guidance and maps the size of bed sheets. And to make matters worse, his navigator (my mum) was more interested in solving crossword puzzles than giving clear directions.

When my dad set off that morning he looked as grim as death. My friend, Janet, looks like that now and she's only facing SPAG, which is shorter but can be just as scarily confusing to the uninitiated as a complicated road network. Her granddaughter, Jemima, is staying for the weekend and she's brought her English homework. 'Her teacher says it will help with her end of year tests,' says Janet. She checks the grammar police aren't hiding behind the sofa and (without a hint of irony) adds, 'Only it's like a foreign language to me.'

She follows me into the kitchen where I put the kettle on. 'SPAG is just an acronym used by teachers,' I explain. 'It's short for spelling, punctuation and grammar.' Janet is not convinced. She thinks I don't appreciate the complexity of the task in hand. In the end I give in and ask her what little Jemima is expected to do.

'Demonstrative determiners.' Janet announces it like someone revealing a top-secret code that only a few tech-savvy maths geniuses could ever hope to crack. 'According to this help sheet, "Determiners go before nouns and there are four kinds: articles, quantifiers, demonstratives and possessives."'

Although I'm a fully trained primary teacher with access to the latest educational jargon, I'm suddenly at a loss. It reminds me of the time Professor Brian Cox tried to make quantum theory available to the masses. I still wouldn't know what wave-particle duality was if it turned up at our door with an identity badge pinned to its lapel. Since then I've been happy to let atoms get on with their job while I get on with mine. But primary English *is* my job.

A proper look at what little Jemima is *actually* expected to do helps us negotiate the fear and confusion that comes when giant clod-hopping terms trample through the garden of common sense and flatten everyday understanding. 'She just has to choose words from the list below and put them into the sentences so that they make sense.' I pour troubled water onto calming teabags and squidge them with a teaspoon.

'So *this, that, these and those* are demonstrative determiners,' says Janet. There is a pause. 'Then what are *articles, quantifiers* and *possessives*?'

'I don't have a defibrillator so best not to ask,' I reply.

Summer term views

12

Know your limits

28th June 2013

With last year's 2012 London Olympics still fresh in my mind and with a summer holiday in Greece just around the corner, I have redoubled my efforts at the gym. One of the core values of our school is to *Aim High*, so I am aiming for male physical perfection. It is a tough journey but when I stop in mid bicep curl to admire the Adonis-like figure staring back at me from the wall mirror it is clear that a combination of aspiration, perspiration and several tubs of whey protein can pay huge dividends.

For a while I gaze transfixed in speechless admiration at the sight of rippling abdominals under a tight-fitting Lycra vest; at the perfect vee made by thrusting deltoids tapering to a trim waist. Adjectives alone cannot describe the powerful quadriceps, the tumescent calves, the rock-like pectorals and the glorious glutes. This is what Michelangelo's David would have looked like if he'd been sponsored by Adidas.

I shift my gaze slightly so that I am no longer staring directly at the man standing next to me, who I think might be contemplating punching my lights out. Now seeing us side by side I am reminded of the film Twins. Only one of us looks like Arnold Schwarzenegger and it's not me. But does the fact that I'm twelve inches too short and bulge in all the wrong places mean that I can never hope to reach the pinnacle of athletic distinction?

Maria, my German personal trainer (who has a never-say-die attitude to extending my fitness levels even to the point where I actually think I might die) must have wondered this herself. I told her in my interview that my targets were to tone up my muscles, improve my body image and wow the ladies at the hotel pool by strutting around in flip flops and a pair of budgie smugglers. The shadow of doubt that flitted across her face briefly dulled her healthy glow. The radiant effects of her energising facial scrub faded.

It is good to know that even the likes of Maria are subject to moments of self-doubt. It makes me feel better about having a mild panic attack when I am advised that a child who nature and nurture have conspired against in terms of reaching intellectual prominence must make a leap in attainment equivalent to conquering Everest without oxygen.

'Surely there has to be some sense of realism,' I tell my wife after collapsing beside her on the settee following a gruelling cardio-workout. 'Are we not all individually bound by our physical and intellectual limits? Are we not just victims of natural de-selection? I can never be Michael Phelps just like Bradley can never be Einstein.'

My wife sighs, 'No and I'm never going to look like Nicole Kidman.' In the interests of marital harmony I resist the temptation to agree with her. She is reading a glossy magazine and has stopped to contemplate an advert for a skin-firming moisturiser that will make aging a thing of the past.

'I liked the world before they banned negativity,' I say. 'Life was a lot easier when you could express doubt, give up after three attempts, and generally opt for the line of least resistance. Too much positivity can be a dangerous thing, you know. It encourages those who *clearly can't* to believe they *actually can.*'

Maria's self-doubt turns out to be a fleeting one. At our next session she demonstrates a renewed sense of purpose by increasing the speed and incline on my treadmill. I try to suggest to her that it might be a good idea if we reduced expectations but all I can do is gasp.

Summer term views

13

Jamie and his bicycle were hell on wheels

22nd April 2016

I examine my newly acquired bruise in detail. It is livid and so am I. 'Of course I'm angry!' I tell my wife. 'It was like being a traffic policeman assigned to the busiest intersection in Mumbai during the Ganesh festival. Believe me there are only so many things you can do with a teacher's whistle and creating order out of traffic chaos is not one of them.'

I breathe deeply, roll my trouser leg down and reflect on the fact that I'm lucky to be alive. An hour ago my continued mortality looked unlikely when I found myself at the mercy of a swarm of lunatic gadabouts. They came at me from all directions; the recklessly speeding and the carelessly ambling; the violently aggressive and the dangerously dithering. I blew my Acme Thunderer until I became lightheaded but nobody took any notice.

This nightmare situation was not envisaged when, in a moment of inspired genius (bordering on insanity) Miss Spry came up with the idea for an after-school Cycle, Scoot and Skate session. At first only the positives were considered. *Think how it will promote healthy outdoor exercise? Imagine how it will defeat the impending obesity crisis? Contemplate how it might help keep death off the road?* Yeah, by confining it to our school playground.

Anyway, before you could say multi-vehicle pile-up, wheels were put in motion. A risk assessment was hastily drawn up and detailed plans were in place. In the interests of safety we decided one section of the playground would be allocated to bicycles and another section to every other mode of transport including scooters, skateboards, roller blades and trainers with ball bearings in them. A third section would be coned off for the exclusive use of the nervous and tentative aka potential road kill.

Outside the school gates (hidden amongst parents) a flock of personal injury lawyers gathered for the feast. They were clearly aware of two factors our risk assessment had overlooked. Firstly, the maximum length of time a child on wheels is able to put safety instructions ahead of the lure of open tarmac is less than three minutes. Secondly, no separate provision had been put in place for Jamie.

Jamie's bike is too big for him. It used to be his dad's and he's not scheduled to grow into it until 2022. Other risk factors included an absence of brakes, two flat tyres and handlebars not aligned with the direction of travel. It was a playground traffic accident waiting to happen, and once Jamie got in the saddle (almost) we knew the waiting was nearly over.

Like the first bumble bee of spring that defies logic in order to perform feats of aerobatic wonder, Jamie took to the open playground on two wheels. It was a wobbly and possibly (given the proximity of crossbar and groin) painful start. But once he got going and began to feel the wind in his face there was literally no stopping him. Boundaries were ignored, walls were blundered into and all intelligent life forms veered out of his way. Unfortunately my reactions are not what they were.

Summer term views

14

Got you

14th June 2013

I drive to the barrier at the end of the car park, press the button and wait. I am leaving early this evening to begin putting my escape plan into operation. This time next year, instead of crawling down the corridor in a last gasp bid to make it to the end of summer term, I will be jetting off to Barbados. Instead of inputting data into countless spreadsheets and writing end-of-year reports I will be lying on a sun-kissed Caribbean beach sipping Bacardi and lime and watching the sun fail to set on my global empire.

This is because a unique business opportunity has presented itself. It all started a few weeks ago when I read that a man called Dave Evans had developed a *Cat Nav,* an ultra-light GPS system that tracks a cat's nocturnal wanderings and allows them to be mapped on a computer. Its purpose is to let pet owners with an unhealthy interest in feline habits see exactly which ginger tom brutally violated poor Fluffy in the shrubbery.

Not having a cat of my own I thought no more about it until this morning when Brandon went missing. He disappeared after we discussed the ins and outs of him not having a playtime until his maths was finished. I argued for in but he went for out, and showing a turn of speed my arthritic ankle and depreciating reflexes were clearly no match for he legged it across the playing field.

A long and fruitless search eventually led me to the Adventure Play Area where, on the path that leads from the Jungle Trek to the Wicker Wigwam, I experienced a revelation of immensely lucrative proportions. It suddenly occurred to me that what I was in most need of right now was something that could easily become the most sought after piece of teacher equipment since the Acme Thunderer.

By the time I got back into school to report Brandon's disappearance my marketing strategy was mentally completed. *Calling all headteachers! Are you intimidated by ever complex safeguarding legislation? Does the threat of a massive negligence claim keep you awake at night? Is the ability of small children to evade barriers, climb walls and outwit the manufacturers of child-proof security fencing worrying you to the point of desperation?*

Install the BRAT NAV Pupil Tracking System today and enjoy the benefits of always knowing the precise whereabouts of even the most elusive pupils. For a modest fee you will be able to pinpoint the exact position of missing minors in moments. Simply enter a child's unique code into your laptop, tablet or smart phone and track his or her movements in real time.

I don't mind admitting that I have been in a state of feverish excitement for most of the day, and now the end of school is here I am the first one out of the building. Unfortunately I am not yet out of the car park. I press the button a second time and the intercom crackles to life. 'Sorry, Mr Eddison, but you are not allowed to leave,' says a familiar and slightly tetchy voice.

My surprise quickly gives way to resolution. The likes of Henry Ford, Bill Gates and Thomas Edison (no relation) would never allow a mere security barrier to stand in the way of commercial success, and neither will I. 'Let me out immediately,' I cry. 'I have a business plan to put together, funding to arrange and a top level conference with the Patents Office to organise.'

'Really?' says the familiar voice, 'Well unfortunately you also have an emergency, after-school meeting to attend. It's on the subject of pupil safeguarding. And it's your fault we're having it so get back in here now!'

Summer term views

15

A merciful mishap

17th April 2015

'Laughing at Aleesha for falling off her chair is not kind; she might have been hurt. You should never take pleasure in the misfortune of others,' I tell my students. Then I fail to act on my own advice by adding, somewhat peevishly, 'Mind you, no one would have reason to laugh at her if she hadn't been rocking backwards on it, would they?'

'Laugh, and the world laughs with you; weep and you weep alone,' said poet Ella Wheeler Wilcox. But what she should have said is weep and the world laughs even more. For it is a well-known fact that nothing is more uplifting to the human spirit than the knowledge that someone else is less fortunate than you are. The misery of others always helps to put our own suffering into perspective.

It is nearing the end of a long day and Aleesha is not the only one feeling sorry for herself. So are all the teachers.

Even now they are looking around their classrooms in the same way that earthquake survivors look around the ruins of their homes. With a heavy heart each one gazes upon a scene of devastation. All about them are unruly piles of unmarked books; torn displays in need of emergency repair; bookcases in desperate disarray; and a sink area that should be cordoned off with hazard warning tape until the Environment Agency arrives.

Get on top of things lest things get on top of you is the golden rule of being a primary teacher. But applying it is another matter. Two hours of determined effort after the children have gone home would easily put things right, but it just isn't going to happen. For by then we will have abandoned our classrooms and taken that weary journey to the Twilight Zone (aka the school hall) to have our teaching improved.

Replacing one training day with a couple of after-hours *twilight* training sessions seemed like a good idea when we were planning the school diary back at the beginning of the year. It seemed an even better idea when we were enjoying that extra Christmas shopping day in December. It seems less good now, at the fag end of a tiring day in class.

The future as far as this evening is concerned looks bleak. Then just two minutes before the end of school a miracle occurs when a message arrives from the office. Joy leaps like a salmon against the tide of despondency. In capital letters on a thin strip of paper are the words TWILIGHT TRAINING CANCELLED. The word CANCELLED has been underlined to reinforce our belief that good things do happen to ordinary teachers.

It is not until later that we discover the awful truth. Our happiness comes at the expense of someone else's misery.

Ms Boudicca (our headteacher) has written her car off and can't get into school. It is miserable news indeed. And while it is tempered by the fact she is uninjured, my reaction was never justified. Punching the air and yelling *get in there you beauty* was simply the wrong thing to do.

Summer term views

16

Goodnight, sleep tight, don't let the killer bugs bite

6th May 2016

Alfie reads aloud from his report. 'Did you know that using bio … logical agents to infect people is not new? Over two and a half thousand years ago the Ass … Ass … Ass-syrians used a fungus called … rye … ergot … to poison their enemy's water supply and *eeurgh…*' He is cut off mid-sentence by a devastating pre-emptive strike.

Earlier our study of micro-organisms had faltered. The children lost interest in 'good bacteria'. The wonders of yeast, that had once risen so promisingly, sagged. The miracle of probiotic yoghurts disappeared down the long and winding digestive tract of educational overload. Resistance to antibiotics was becoming all too evident. The only remedy was large doses of excruciating pain, hideous disfigurement and death.

Killer Bugs is the sort of headline guaranteed to raise temperatures and set pulses racing. In no time at all a selection of weirdly exotic names (staphylococcus, streptococcus, E. coli, etc.) caused an outbreak of morbid curiosity in bad bacteria. This in turn led to a spike in interest in the terrible diseases infections can cause. What child is immune to graphic descriptions of smallpox, necrotising fasciitis and Black Death?

Cartoon illustrations of evil bugs grinning maliciously out of primary text books gave way to the glare of full colour photographs of the real thing splashed across an interactive whiteboard. Giant tadpole-like strains of tetanus; worm-shaped clostridium botulinum; long writhing strands of bacillus anthracis. And once exposed to these magnified images the children grew feverish for more.

But size isn't everything. Or is it? In the time it takes one bacterium to become two the children forgot these alien life-forms are actually microscopically small. Enlarging them only enhanced their repulsive lure and affirmed their existence. A positive side effect of this was that I could reveal the awful truth in the most dramatic way possible. 'Did you know there are millions of similar bacteria living right now on your hands?'

Disbelief turned to denial. Children examined their palms in detail. The anti-bacterial gel was suddenly in demand. How is it possible for vast colonies of germs to live on such small (albeit slightly scruffy) areas of skin? I ignored their questions and pressed home the learning advantages. 'It's not just your hands either. They also live up your nose, Anjelica... There are billions in your digestive system, Jamie ... They are in the very air that you breathe, Dyson ... And you won't believe how many are in William's saliva from sucking the end of his ruler.'

When the gagging, the choking and the expressions of disgust died down, I set the children their task. Armed only with a few tablet computers, some text books and an assortment of photocopied information sheets, I gave them forty five minutes to seek out, isolate and investigate Killer Bugs. When their mission was accomplished a select group of researchers were invited to reveal their findings.

Alfie's investigation into the deadly secrets of biological warfare was a popular choice, but sinister forces sought to silence him. Why else would William fire spit from the end of a plastic ruler?

Summer term views

17

Beard and wonderful

1st May 2015

It is summer term and the thoughts of our female teachers turn to *fifty shades of grey*. 'That's what my wife calls it,' I tell them in reference to the patchwork of hairiness around the bottom half of my face. Before anyone can respond our headteacher appears. She is investigating reports that a scruffy-looking old man has been spotted wandering the corridors.

'Well that's one mystery solved,' she says, brightly. 'So, Mr Eddison, I see you're now sporting a beard.' I smooth my bristles and smile winningly. Facial hair is in fashion at the moment, and the colour of mine is not entirely dissimilar to George Clooney's.

'Some of the mums couldn't keep their eyes off me this morning,' I announce with a wink.

'They probably couldn't believe someone as old as you is still a teacher,' laughs Miss Brightsmile, which is ironic because she looks too young to be one.

'Just because I didn't want to join in your game of *duck, duck, goose*, doesn't mean I'm no longer up to the job,' I protest. 'I have an arthritic right ankle; a terrible legacy from my sporting past. I used to play Sunday League football you know.'

Looking around it occurs to me that the age profile of our staff has got dramatically younger over recent years. Later I discover it is not a phenomenon confined to this school. According to an OECD study carried out in 2013 Britain has the youngest primary teachers in the developed world. Almost a third of them are under the age of thirty.

Maybe they're conducting a witch-hunt against aging teachers? Once upon a time grey hairs were revered as a sign of wisdom. Now they are nothing but symbols of physical degeneration, mental decline and an inability (or unwillingness) to use information technology to maximise pupil learning. From now on I will keep a suspicious eye on these bright young things that have taken over our staffroom. In time I will discover what they really think of my generation.

Until then I will rely solely on my children to tell it like it is. 'Did you know you've got a beard, Mr Eddison?' says Ryan, who probably thinks I just forgot to shave.

'Yeah, how does it make me look?' I ask.

He reflects for a while as though I might be asking him a trick question. 'Really old … like about forty two,' he replies.

'I was hoping you would say that, Ryan, because I'm growing it to play the part of a very old man in a famous play called The Crucible.' He wants to know what it's about so I explain. 'It's a true story based on some terrible events that happened in a town called Salem in 1692. Lots of people are accused of witchcraft and sentenced to death, and unfortunately my wife is one of them.'

Light dawns. 'Oh so that's why you need a beard; because you're a *wizard*!' exclaims Ryan.

I put an arm around him and whisper, 'Listen, don't repeat this in case it leads to a hysterical reaction, but my real name is *Hairy* Potter.'

Summer term views

18

The curse of the mummy

31st May 2013

The remains of the sarcophagus of Tutankhamen are shocking to see. The painted death mask is crushed beyond recognition; the bandages that contained his three-thousand-year-old remains are draped across the bookcase; the gruesome contents of several Canopic jars have been scattered over the floor. Was this a deliberate act of sabotage or could it be the Curse?

The mystery of how the remains of the boy king were defiled will have to wait. Niall has self-esteem issues and however this act of desecration came about it has caused him untold emotional damage. I poke what is left of the death mask into nothing like its original shape. 'I think we can fix this.'

My words have the desired effect. He stops head butting the wall. 'When?' says Niall.

'When what?' I reply.

He turns a hot, tear-stained face in my direction. 'When can we fix my fucking sarcophagus?'

In the interests of circumventing physical damage to Niall (and structural damage to the building) I promise that if he refrains from swearing we will repair it during lunchtime. I neglect to tell him that my lunchtime already has an evil curse of prior importance hanging over it. All week an ancient threat has haunted my thoughts: *update your pupil assessments, Mr Eddison, or face disciplinary procedures.*

Pie crust promises are not what you make to children like Niall. I should have been straight with him, and said, 'Look, there are times when life is just not pharaoh, okay? I mean shit happens. It's a fact. Get over it.' But I didn't, and now I am riven with guilt. It is a guilt compounded by a fond memory of Mr Kettlewell.

'Don't worry, lad, we can rebuild it. We can put it back together again as good as new,' said Mr Kettlewell after Fred Butcher sank the Ark Royal in a fit of nautical jealousy. Obviously it wasn't the real Ark Royal. Even Fred Butcher would have found it a challenge to sink a thirty-seven-thousand-ton aircraft carrier.

The Ark Royal in question was mine. I had painstakingly crafted it out of interlocking fag packets and papier mache over a series of Friday afternoons in the sixties. Fred Butcher said it looked more like the Bismarck and peremptorily stamped on it in the national interest.

I have no doubt that if such a violation were to happen today it would shatter my self-esteem and leave me emotionally and behaviourally challenged. But the sixties was another place and a unique sense of optimism prevailed.

After all it was only twenty years since my grandad had won the war. TB was coughing its last, polio was kicking off its leg braces and antibiotics were beating the hell out of bacterial infections.

Nothing could dent my confidence in Mr Kettlewell's ability to reconstruct the Ark Royal. The future was assured. James Bond would forever keep the world safe from the likes of Auric Goldfinger. Doctor Who had successfully thwarted The Dalek Invasion of the Earth. And two days earlier I had kissed Brenda Watson behind the bike shed.

Today, however, a brooding tension fills my lunchtime classroom. I speak in whispers, urging Niall to wrap bandages around Tutankhamen's body in silence. My delicate task to fix the death mask while simultaneously entering pupil data into the system begins.

But only a few seconds have ticked by when I am interrupted by a bloodcurdling scream. It is followed by the unravelled remains of a long dead pharaoh levitating through the air at great speed. An instant later I come face to face with the Curse of the Niall. 'I don't fucking want to! It's fucking crap! That's why I fucking smashed it up!'

Summer term views

19

Never give up on the grey kids

13th August 2010

Ten years ago a friend of ours gave birth to a baby boy. Jake was two months premature and seriously ill. My wife went to see him for what she thought would be the only time. He was not expected to survive the night. Even the dedicated staff at the specialist baby care unit had given up on him.

'It's terrible,' she sobbed over the telephone. 'I've never seen anything so pathetic. He's so tiny he would fit in the palm of my hand, and the worst thing is he has no colour. He's grey; almost transparent. You can see his tiny organs flickering beneath his skin. And you know that very soon he will give in completely and his little life will be snuffed out like a candle.'

Sometimes you have to fight and kick and scream in order to survive. And sometimes, if you can't do it for yourself, somebody has to do it for you. Jake's mother did just that and somehow she galvanised everybody including Jake and his team of carers into renewed effort. Ten years later I am pleased to announce that Jake can fight and kick and scream for himself.

But what about Rogan? He arrived in our school a couple of years ago after several other schools had given up on him. No one looking from the outside would have put money on him surviving for very long with us either. Rogan is a grey child. You can tell grey children because they look ... well ... *grey*. It comes from years of never having had a proper wash, never eating a healthy diet and never getting a good night's sleep. It comes from hanging around grey streets until the grey hours, and consorting with grey people who inhabit the grey margins of a grey council estate.

There is no obvious incentive for tough schools like ours to nurture its grey children. With barely surmountable floor targets looming ahead of us and the hounds of Ofsted closing in behind, the last thing we need are children who will make learning even more difficult for themselves and everybody around them. If we were cynical our best hope would be that they will either drift through the system like grey ghosts and leave no trace other than a few poor percentage points, or that they will scream, kick, rant and swear their way to a pupil referral unit.

Rogan remained with us until he left at the end of Year Six. His SATs scores were not good and his contribution to that grim ledger of attainment was a negative one. In truth by the time he came to our school he was already damaged goods; unfit for the purpose of achieving in line with National Expectations, and if we were in the *business* of education, no one could have blamed us for doing our damn best to return him under the Sale of Goods Act.

Fortunately for Rogan we don't give up on grey children. For us Every Child Matters. Every child who screams, kicks, rants and swears at us matters. Every child who because of the shit hand life has dealt them treats us like shit still matters. They matter because we may be the nearest thing to a family they've ever known, and our care for them must be unconditional.

Rogan came to the Leaver's Party looking significantly less grey. He wore a suit staff had bought for him and a grin that was priceless. After all, it's good to bring a little colour into this dull, data-obsessed education system of ours, isn't it?

Summer term views

20

Sun turns star-crossed lovers crazy

6th August 2010

From the outset there was something dangerously romantic about those last days of summer term. I don't mean the sweet allure of six weeks holiday. Neither do I mean the mental image of a bikini-clad Miss Gorgeous lying sun-bronzed on the beach at Lanzarote; although for the rest of this paragraph I'm going to take a few deep breaths…

What most aroused my fears was the way Year Six became suddenly enamoured by thoughts of love. It is scary indeed to observe eleven-year-old boys spraying themselves with enough Eau de Testosterone to beguile a female rhinoceros. It is even more scary to see eleven-year-old girls – on the pretext of having grown out of their uniforms – wearing too little of everything but make-up.

The cold days toiling under the shadow of SATs were clearly a thing of the past. Announcing our best results ever raised barely a flicker of excitement (except in the head's office where loud whoops were heard as she performed cartwheels, ate Belgian chocolates and drank copious quantities of pink champagne). Year Six had other, more important matters to obsess about.

Some say the fierce sun went to their heads. Others blame the cruel whispers that emanated from behind the bike racks. Several more point the finger at Mother Nature whose reckless fecundity had turned the wild area into a warren of intimate hideaways. Knowing the cause, however, is of little consequence when it cannot change what happened. For never was a story of more woe than this of Britney and her Robbie-O!

What started with a peck on the lips, quickly progressed to a smack in the mouth and ended with a mass brawl the like of which has not been seen since a famous family in Verona thought it might be a good idea to gate-crash a party thrown by its neighbours from hell.

Britney and Nathan were an item. They lived next door to each other; their parents were best friends; they had been in love since they were three. Numerous missives, intercepted as they passed around the classroom, bore testimony to this. The only pity is that they bore little testimony to the ability of either correspondent to use compound sentences, adverbial phrases, a variety of logical connectives and the truth; for Britney secretly loved another.

Apparently, while Nathan had been re-sculpting his hair in the boys' toilets during the Leavers' Party, Robbie, his arch enemy from the parallel Year Six class had stolen his girlfriend's heart. They had checked each other out across a crowded hall and danced the Macarena together. The next day Britney sent several messages via her best friend Emma and a secret rendezvous was arranged. It took place under cover of the wild area.

It is not a best kept secret that best friends are not best at keeping secrets. Within moments of that first tentative kiss, Nathan arrived hot on the scene swearing to make worm's meat out of Robbie. And because news of a good fight travels much faster than your average lunchtime supervisor, lots of other children arrived hot on the scene too, and for several minutes all hell broke loose. By the time order was restored Robbie had sustained several bruises, Nathan's hair was in desperate need of gel and Britney's inconsolable screams had provoked breathing difficulties.

Summer term views

21

Staggering on to the bitter end

5th August 2011

A silence descends over the dusty arena that is the school playing field. Confrontation is in the air. Nerves twitch and muscles tense. The world grinds steadily to a halt. There is no going back now. Control your breathing. Try to relax. Maintain focus. Get ready and…

An explosion shocks the world into action. The chase is on. The baying and whooping of the crowd is barely audible amid the pounding of feet and the gasping for breath. And though I try with several fibres of my being to keep up with the pack, it is no use. I am hopelessly lost – or rather last. Ignominy, humiliation and ridicule will be my fate.

To be honest, I'm not the athlete I imagine I once was, and the blue riband highlight of our school's sports day – the staff one hundred metre dash – can no longer be classed as my best event. In the time it takes me to travel twenty metres up the track the race is already over. The sight of a young, irritatingly athletic and in every sense dashing Mr Twist grinning handsomely at his adoring fans and pausing to make Usain Bolt poses for the cameras takes the wind out of my lungs and leaves me gasping at the sheer unfairness of the aging process.

Of course that's the problem, isn't it? I'm not getting any younger. The years are not only catching up with me they're overtaking me, giving me the rods and telling me to *get off the road grandad*. And while I might like King Canute – or Cnut as those with a taste for mischievous anagrams prefer to spell him – try to turn back the tide of years, the reality is it's never going to happen.

There is a moment – technically I think it's called *hitting the wall* – when my heart and legs tell me I can go no further. That I should give in now, step off the track and disappear up my own dust trail. But apparently there is no longer provision for this in the rules. The head assures me that continuing to the bitter end is in my contract and cannot be renegotiated.

So with those grainy 1954 images of Jim Peters collapsing out of the Empire Games Marathon in Vancouver on my mind, I slow my pace, shorten my stride pattern and trundle towards what appears to be an ever-receding finish line. There I will accept with equanimity the cruel comments and derisory laughter that accompany failure. There I will acknowledge with smiling good humour the half-hearted clapping and the hollow cheers for having taken part in the first place. There I will, in a spirit of self-mockery, punch the air and strike a celebratory pose.

But of course all that will be on the outside. On the inside I will curse the blight of age-related joint pain, the fibrous adhesions around my knees and the tendinitis in my right ankle. I will curse the frozenness of my left shoulder, the irritability of my bowel and the pain in the arse-ness of my haemorrhoids. I will curse the highness of my blood pressure, the lowness of my testosterone and the spread of my middle-age gut. I will curse the physical and mental toll that too many years trying to keep pace with ever livelier classes of primary-aged children has wrought. But most of all I will curse David Cameron and his proposal to move the age at which teachers can retire so far down the track I'll need a mobility scooter to carry me over it.

Part Four

And breathe…

1

The children had a whale of a time on Filey beach

24th August 2018

Today I notice with some alarm that lots of primary-aged children are being inadequately supervised on the beach. Some are burying their siblings in the sand while others are running squealing into the sea. A few are shivering violently in an effort to maintain core body temperature. 'That boy needs wrapping in a towel,' I tell Mrs Eddison, who in turn reminds me that he's not my responsibility.

We are strolling along the shore at Filey (south of Scarborough) towards a narrow strip of hard rock that juts into the sea to form the northern tip of Filey Bay. This strip of rock is called the Brigg. My friend, Eddie (a retired but very enthusiastic geography teacher) could no doubt explain its geology in minute detail, but the only rock I'm familiar with has Filey written down the middle.

This place has been a favourite since June 1986, when it helped me survive my probationary year. At a time when new teachers were expected to sink or swim, I mostly floundered. Only when someone thought I might be going under for the last time was I offered a lifebelt. 'You'll get brownie points for volunteering to do this,' said Mrs Batty (deputy head and mentor) as we waved goodbye to relieved parents from the coach window.

Taking twenty needy children from a decimated mining community to the seaside for a week promised to be a wonderful opportunity for an enthusiastic young teacher. But the joy of exciting days filled with sea, sand and headcounts was spoiled by long evenings when the tide of excitement ebbed and exposed the dreaded *Filey Diaries*. Persuading children exhausted from *doing stuff* to record the *stuff* they've been *doing* isn't easy.

But Mr Ahab (headteacher) announced their Filey Diaries would be the subject of a school assembly on our return. So when my yawned threats and weary pleas failed to save a puffin colony, a lifeboat station and Whitby Abbey for posterity, I knew I was in trouble. Worn down by responsibility and lack of sleep, the *assembly* started to haunt my horizon like a black-sailed ship. What I needed was something colossal to inspire them.

And what could be more colossal than a whale on Filey Brigg? At least that's what Ryan said it was, and trying to persuade a child who has rarely travelled beyond Rotherham that he's confusing one sea mammal with another is no easy task. In the rush of excitement all my attempts to explain that it wasn't a whale fell on ears deafened by the ocean's roar.

Because a monster from the deep always trumps a probationary teacher's authority, my desperate pleas for everyone to come back went unheeded. With furious waves threatening to drag several young children and my career into the abyss, Mrs Batty finally lost patience and blew her whistle. 'Get your clipboards out, sit on your bottoms and write about it,' she snapped.

When his diary account left Mr Ahab confused as to whether he'd really seen a whale on Filey Brigg, Ryan grudgingly admitted the truth. 'Turns out it were nowt but a dead seal.'

And breathe...

2

On safari with the real minibeasts

12th August 2011

Well what did you expect, a herd of wildebeest thundering across the Serengeti in a race of life or death? Alligators brooding menacingly along the banks of the Orinoco before launching themselves with unrivalled ferocity to snap up an unsuspecting gazelle? A slobbering pack of bloody hyena tearing greedily at the still warm carcass of a baby giraffe?

Angelika scratches her head and looks bored. Our Wild Garden Safari is not the wonderfully inspiring, totally hands-on, real life experience I had anticipated. The only excitement comes when Ryan puts a spider down the back of Emma's frock and her screams send every living creature in a three-mile radius scurrying for cover.

Of course I blame that Attenborough bloke. Minibeasts are just not as exciting as they used to be. I know size isn't everything but how is half a dozen bewildered woodlice under a house brick ever going to compare with a fully HD rhinoceros bearing down on you from a fifty-four-inch flat-screen home entertainment system?

The problem is I am competing with a virtual world whose ever extending three dimensional tentacles are tearing children further and further away from mundane reality. I am in Mortal Kombat with the world of Play Station. The Nintendo Wii leaves me breathless and exhausted. I am on a treadmill that goes ever faster, ever nowhere, in a race that cannot be won. The expectations on children to have a work ethic are diminished; the expectations on me to keep them constantly engaged and constantly learning are increased. And to keep me honest I must be ever under the observation spotlight [gasp] a specimen under the microscope of those in charge of quality control [gasp] a helpless, squirming victim under the great beady-eye of the magnifying glass of… Ah?

Magnifying glasses improve the overall experience no end as they bring the life and death dramas of this quiet backwater of our school's playground to stark life. The humble ladybird instantly reveals itself to be a giant, trundling predator capable of devouring an entire colony of aphids in a single sitting. Columns of ants organise themselves into a ruthless red army bent on world domination. Bumble bees, fully laden, throb like apache helicopters among the thistles. Coy butterflies, like painted geishas, brazenly spread their wings.

Angelika is still scratching her head, but by and large our safari is going really well. Then Bradley uses his lens to sacrifice a worm and Daisy, sobbing loudly at the cruel injustice of it all, threatens to report him to the Animal

Liberation Front who, she reliably informs everyone, will torch his house, throw acid in his face and put a bomb under his dad's Ford Escort.

She sobs even louder when he tries to set fire to her too. At this point the term *safeguarding* begins to trumpet like a distressed elephant inside my head. Should I have written a risk assessment for a Wild Garden Safari? It's not just Daisy's imminent immolation that concerns me. What would be the implications if someone turned out to be allergic to nettles or ant bites or bee stings? What if somebody went into anaphylactic shock?

'Remember, children, that everywhere is a habitat for something,' I explain from the comparative safety of my classroom. 'Now for your homework I want you to check out your backyards, search your sheds and explore the cupboard under the stairs. Remember, anywhere can be a habitat.'

'Can Angelika's head be a habitat?' asks Ryan, searching through her tangled locks (not with a fine-tooth comb although that might come later). 'Only there's some minibeasts crawling through her undergrowth.'

And breathe…

3

Lessons from the odd couple

27th August 2010

I always go for my annual health check in August, that way I can expect a low enough blood pressure reading to convince myself I'll survive the next eleven months. Doctor Rains was new to the practice. He looked up at me and grinned, 'Mr Eddison? Now that name rings a bell.'

'Never heard that one before,' I replied. Then I realised he was being serious. A few seconds later it dawned on me who he was. And the realisation instantly took me back to my probationary year.

I began teaching in 1988 having spent twelve years in an engineering factory and four as a mature student. The school, on a rundown council estate, was not dissimilar from the one I went to; except where *we* sang *Jerusalem* every morning this one rang to the tune of *Come and have a go if you think you're hard enough.* And I may not have been hard enough if it hadn't been for Marigold and Richard.

Marigold, the deputy head, was the Daily Mail disguised as House & Garden. Middle-aged and middle class, she wore flowery dresses over bullet-proof corsetry and perfume fierce enough to ward off the least adequately toilet trained. Her home was in the west of Sheffield where posh people live and where, in the city's industrial heyday, the prevailing wind brusquely wafted away the smoke and stench of vulgar industrial toil.

Marigold modelled the rules – actually I interpreted them as guidelines – for surviving the trials of classroom life. She refused point blank to tie the damp shoelaces of little boys returning from the toilets. She had cupboards more regimented than a Sandhurst passing out parade. And she sailed serenely through the urgent needs of small children like the QE2 ploughing through a flotilla of bobbing dinghies.

Unfortunately she also modelled what not to do. Like whenever Ryan scratched in his English book something that resembled a motorway pile up, or ate his dinner with his fingers, or climbed on the school roof and threw tiles at the caretaker, she would shake her head and say, 'What do you expect from children round here?' And whenever Zoe bit someone, or stole their pencil case, or was over generous with her head lice, she would raise her eyebrows and declare, 'But really, you can't expect anything better from children round here.' And when she said these things I would force a smile and say to myself, 'But I came from *round here.* Or from somewhere very similar.'

Richard came from *round here* too. His age and

background were identical to those of Ryan and Zoe. But in terms of expectations he taught me a quite different lesson.

'*Actually,* Mr Eddison,' he said, while I was demonstrating with several different sized balls how the solar system is arranged, 'Venus is nearer the Sun than Earth, and Mars is further away. And *actually*, Mr Eddison, you need to swap Saturn and Jupiter around. And *actually*, Mr Eddison, I don't think you know your Asteroids from Uranus.'

Actually, Richard was right and he spent the rest of the year advising me on such things as the difference between pollination and fertilisation, why planes don't fall out of the sky and how to switch the bloody computer on.

Looking back, I suppose Richard had at least one thing in common with Marigold; self-belief of the armour-plated variety. And that made him resistant to both the restraints of social deprivation and other people's low expectations. Which I suppose explains why he's where he is today: assessing my fitness to survive another year of teaching.

And breathe…

4

Summer holidays are all about feeding the beast

10th August 2018

Right now Maisie doesn't know the Beast in the corner will devour her. Her existence will be terminated and her identity erased. In short she will be chewed thoroughly, swallowed entirely and excreted as unidentifiable waste matter. Maisie's mum will meet the same fate, as will her dad, both hamsters and her cat called Missy. The beast in the corner is merciless and all consuming.

He was delivered by transit van shortly after 9.00 am. Though the labelling on the box suggested he came from a South American rainforest he is in fact Korean. The labelling referred to a well-known on-line retailer. Within minutes he was installed in a corner of our garage and hungry to begin his tasks. I smiled briefly and forced him to eat his own packaging.

The Beast is a heavy duty shredder for home and office use. He comes with a twelve-month guarantee, a twenty-three-litre-capacity bin, durable steel blades and a diet that includes staff training hand-outs, marked test sheets, annotated progress reviews and draft reports to parents. He can also stomach more resilient items including unwanted CDs and overused credit cards.

This makes him the ideal companion for the first week of my school holiday. While Mrs Eddison slaves in the sullen heat of a busy city centre solicitors, I relax in a cool corner of the garage and feed the Beast pile after pile of unwanted (but possibly sensitive) school detritus. In an era when the irresistible force of data protection meets the immovable mountain of information overload, feeding the Beast is a fun and useful way for a teacher to enjoy his summer.

At least it is until I open a manila document wallet marked CHILDREN'S FACT FILES and find Maisie's at the top. Reading it for the first time since last September, brings back several happy memories individually wrapped in the warm glow of nostalgia. The morning she swam her first width of the pool without armbands. The day she was named Star of the Week in our Sparkle and Shine Assembly. The time her nose finally stopped bleeding after more than an hour.

It is with reluctance that I send her to meet a grizzly fate in the belly of the Beast, but by the time Ben and his five siblings have been ingested it's getting easier. Gary, his sister and his grandad with one leg are swiftly followed by Sade, Troy and Jazeera. Even the A3 sheet with a smiling class photograph at the top and a single statement from each child describing what they hope the year might bring (but mostly didn't) disappears without a fight.

By mid-afternoon my urge to feed the Beast overrides my emotional attachment to children's memories. In a frenzy he devours their stories, their pentomino investigations and their attempts to identify subordinate clauses. His hunger grows apace and my increasingly desperate efforts to satisfy it only cease when Mrs Eddison comes home from work. Recognizing the crazed look in my eyes, she calmly unplugs the Beast from the socket. 'Now go and put the kettle on,' she says with a sigh.

And breathe…

5

On the road

7th August 2015

Inspired by the Yorkshire stages of last year's Tour de France I recently took up cycling. 'It will be good for my health and good for the environment,' I explained to my wife, neglecting to mention that it would also be good for transporting me away from her *School Holiday to do list*. 'And of course it won't cost anything! There is no charge for the wind in your face and the freedom of the open road under your wheels.'

Actually there was an initial investment of £499.99 for a basic road bike. Mine is of a lightweight alloy construction with sixteen gears making it suitable for every gradient. So far I seem to be getting by with the one gear that allows me to go very slowly uphill while pedalling like the clappers. I suspect I will only need my dual pivot calliper brakes and nerves of steel to go down the other side.

As the heroes of Le Tour know only too well, Sheffield is surrounded by hills. For example, to get from my house to the picturesque beauty of the nearby Peak District National Park involves first ascending two especially steep roads before turning left onto the A625 Hathersage Road. This in turn winds its way relentlessly uphill for 3.9 miles before finally achieving the breath-taking heights of Burbage Moor.

Breath-taking is a particularly apt description because by the time I reach the highest point mine is all gone. While I stop and wait for it to catch up I enjoy the scenery. It reminds me of when the hectic last days of summer term gave way to the wide open calm of six weeks of freedom. City streets have been replaced by moorland. Ahead of me are big skies, spectacular views and a glorious four-mile descent to the village of Hathersage with its selection of welcoming pubs.

I resist the urge to shout yippee ki-yay and content myself with being a focussed blur of multi-coloured sporting excellence zooming down freedom's highway. I was introduced to the colourful world of essential cycling accessories by the same man who sold me my bike. 'A hi-vis helmet and performance sunglasses are essential safety equipment,' he said. 'Now what about some proper clothing?'

Apparently *compression clothing improves performance during endurance exercise by optimising the muscles' oxygen usage.* He handed me some matching fluorescent shorts and a top. 'Lycra fits snugly, has excellent aerodynamic qualities and is quick drying. And with a colourful design like this one you'll be guaranteed to turn heads.'

I certainly drew the attention of my neighbours this morning, though I suspect their good-natured heckling and cries of 'Get off and milk it, grandad,' were born of jealousy.

Well they would certainly be jealous now, seeing me sitting outside the Plough Inn at this picturesque Derbyshire beauty spot enjoying a well-earned pint. It is only when my glass turns from being half full to half empty that I remember I have a steep four-mile ascent at the start of my journey back. Maybe I should get on my bike and look for a teaching job in Norfolk?

And breathe…

6

A problem in the bedroom

21st August 2013

'While you're on holiday I need you to do something for me in the bedroom,' says my wife, and my hopes are on the rise. 'I want you to help me strip,' she adds, and they rise even higher. 'Now let's see how imaginative you can be with these.' She waves something provocatively in my direction and I realise my hopes have climaxed prematurely. It is a decorator's colour chart and a book of wallpaper designs. 'Don't look so worried,' she says. 'I've arranged for a man to do the *real work*. I just need you to strip the walls and help me choose paint and paper.'

After thirty five years of marital harmony (with occasional periods of discord, cacophony and shrill jarring sounds) she is fully aware of my inability to do practical things. Unfortunately she is not fully aware of my sensitivity to comments that question my manliness. This is why I am suddenly overwhelmed by an ancient impulse to get my machismo out. 'What do you mean you've arranged for a man to do the *real work*? I'm more than capable of doing a bit of painting and decorating.'

'Well if you think you're up to it I suppose it's not too late to cancel him,' says my wife. She leaves the threat hanging in the air until it becomes clear she's won an argument which up to now I didn't even know we were having.

'Hang on, don't cancel just yet,' I say. 'Obviously I need to check I have the necessary equipment first.'

A cursory look around the garage soon confirms that my tools are no longer up to the job. My brushes have shrivelled away in a mug of white spirit, my nine-inch roller has congealed and my fold-away decorating table is showing signs of erectile dysfunction.

The economics of the situation are such that it will be cheaper to let the decorator do the work. I console myself with the fact that at least I made the offer, and we begin leafing through fifty shades of every colour you can invent a name for. By the simple process of eliminating all my suggestions we arrive at a colour scheme my wife likes. My only task now is to provide the man with tea and professional advice. What can possibly go wrong?

Things come to a head two weeks later when my wife announces that if the bedroom is not finished before I go back to school in September there is a chance we could become a divorce statistic. As she is a member of the legal profession and I have an aversion to spending my twilight years living in a cardboard box insulated with unwanted copies of the TES Jobs section, I grudgingly get my tool box out and contemplate the job in hand.

In front of me is an entire wall of freshly painted wardrobes, cupboards and drawers. A close visual inspection confirms the quality of the painter's craftsmanship. There is not a run, a blemish or even a brushstroke to be seen. Unfortunately there are no handles to be seen either. 'They can't be put back on until the gloss has hardened off,' said the decorator. 'But then I expect your husband here will be able to do that little job himself.'

'I doubt it, he's useless with a screwdriver,' said my wife. It is an opinion the few remaining shreds of my masculinity felt an overwhelming urge to take issue with, and which until now has caused the bedroom to be something of a no-go area.

And breathe…

7

A day at the beach shows creativity is all at sea

2nd August 2016

Mrs Eddison and I are at Runswick Bay on the North Yorkshire Coast. It is early evening and we are enjoying a stroll along the beach. The tide, like most of the families who were here earlier, has slipped away to put its feet up for a few hours and left us to relish the peace and quiet. It's good to feel wet sand on your bare feet. My toes are numb with cold but I suspect the seawater is doing wonders for my athlete's foot.

The odd-looking pebble I pick up and examine was formerly a piece of green glass that has been rounded and made opaque by the action of waves. It looks unusual and feels strangely satisfying to the touch. Already I'm beginning to wonder how I might use it. After all it's illegal for primary teachers to visit the seaside without collecting useful creative resources.

In cupboards, drawers and cardboard boxes; in the loft, in the shed and in the garage; and in countless other places I've forgotten about, they wait to be rediscovered. There are the whelk shells that captured the sadness of the ocean; the dried out starfish that long for regeneration; the tests of sea urchins bloated with dark secrets; sea horses that pulled the coaches of mermaid princesses; and driftwood snakes in suspended petrification.

My seaside resources don't get used much these days. The tide of learning turned and flooded the curriculum with mundane targets. Teachers caught in the rip unexpectedly found themselves floundering. Every attempt to grab the lifeline of the next set of tick boxes left them wearier than before. In deeper waters, creativity long ago lost the struggle to keep from going under. I sigh and put the pebble into my pocket.

It's twilight when we set off along Ellerby Lane towards Whitby and a famous fish and chip shop. It's a journey we made many times when our own children were young. They're grown up now and have moved on, but the sudden recollection catches me in nostalgia's undertow. When did the slowly unravelling lanes of childhood get widened and re-classified? When did they become breathless motorways and crowded intersections, hell bent on rushing us along the Superhighway of Time?

I wonder if my pebble might one day be more than a lump of sea glass. An uncut emerald from a pirate's treasure trove, perhaps? Or a fragment of star that fell to earth as a meteorite? Will there be an opportunity for me to pass it around a group of children and see them marvel at its mysterious inner glow? Will I ever get to watch them witness its strange, pulsating force and imagine what miracles it might perform?

It's dark when we park the car in Whitby town centre and head in the direction of the harbour and the smell of fish and chips. August is buzzing with holidaymakers, and as we thread our way through them I can't help but smile to myself. No one knows that this ordinary teacher is in possession of a most extraordinary object. No one knows I have the power to change the world.

And breathe…

8

Food of Gods can induce vomiting

20th August 2010

I am contemplating Greece's greatest gift to the civilised world, which in my opinion is not the Socratic Method. Neither for that matter is it Democracy, because that gave us Michael Gove. In fact you can stop theorising about Pythagoras, say *screw you* to Archimedes, shout oaths at Hippocrates, debate Plato till the cows come home, and give Jason a swift kick up the Argos. For me, Greece's greatest gift to mankind is edible, incredible and heading my way.

Let me explain that at this precise moment I am sitting on a white plastic garden chair outside a kebab shop in the Cretan town of Chania. My immediate surroundings are not salubrious. These are the outer limits of the town's tourist area. Here the wasps are leaner, meaner and more persistent. There are no handsome young men trying to sell boat rides and the only mopeds around are awaiting repair in Ioannis's garage just across the road. There is, however, a Greek bearing gifts. His name is Stavros, and according to Janet and John (not *the* Janet and John) from Macclesfield, he serves the best gyros pitta ever.

The humble gyros pitta is my Achilles heel. It is the food of Gods. Nothing you can do that doesn't involve at least one other human being and the exchange of bodily fluids comes close to it. A lightly toasted pitta bread caressing succulent slices of gyros meat combined with a tomato and onion salad, generously topped with oodles of creamy, garlicky tzatziki and served with a gentle dusting of paprika. I salivate at the thought ... And then I recall the mess, the terrible cries and the awful stench, and suddenly lose my appetite.

'I'm not eating any of that foreign crap; it'll make me spew!' Aidan announced to the entire class on the day of our Greek Feast. This was the culmination of seven weeks spent studying the cradle of western civilisation: the most influential characters, ideas and events in the history of the world.

'Why not?' I asked.

'There could be anything in it!' he replied, which is not bad coming from a child whose diet normally consists of bright orange nuggets made from a subtle combination of minced chicken skin, mechanically recovered meat slurry, salt, water, bulking agent and a combination of the best flavourings and preservatives the chemical industry can provide.

'Why don't you try this?' I said handing him a green olive on a cocktail stick.

'Are you havin' a laugh?'

I sighed and switched off the bouzouki music. 'Okay, everyone stop what you are doing and look this way. Jordan, do not smear tzatziki on Britney's face. Isabel, put the spoon down and step away from the moussaka. *I said put the spoon down and step away from the moussaka.* Ryan, just because Nathan threw dolmades at you doesn't mean you have to throw them back. Oh and Rogan, don't even think about smashing that plate. Thank you. Now, children, Aidan is reluctant to try food from our Greek menu. Who would like to suggest something they particularly enjoyed? '

'I liked that pink stuff,' said Britney.

Aidan dipped his pitta in the taramasalata. He examined it. He sniffed it. Finally he nibbled it. Then he nibbled some more and all went well until he asked what it was made from. And before I could come up with a convincing lie, Rashid told everyone the truth.

In not much longer than it takes to shriek, '*Fish eggs? Eurgh!*' my entire class had turned vomiting into an Olympic sport.

And the rest, as they say, is history.

And breathe…

9

Down at the bottom of the garden

19th August 2011

Right now I am relaxing on a lounger in the garden of a luxury villa on the Costa Almeria. Where better to celebrate the miracle of our school spectacularly achieving near-impossible targets? Where better to dismiss the implications of upwardly revised targets for the year ahead? Where better to ignore the gathering storm clouds of September and the prospect of inspection under the new framework; where deprivation counts for nothing and Dr Gove's miracle cure for the statistically challenged is academy status?

It doesn't take much for my half-full glass of Sangria to appear half empty, does it? That's because for some reason lazing on a sun lounger can't stop a middle-aged teacher's thoughts turning to the educational implications of Brandon Turner's garden.

Gardens can say a lot about family life. For example our garden confirms Mrs Eddison's view that a man with six weeks to spare should make sure it is a work of art for the two weeks he won't be there to enjoy it. To this end vast quantities of physical and financial resources have been expended.

Of course a lack of financial resources can never be used as an excuse for horticultural underachievement. Blood, sweat and tears combined with resilience to nettle rash and a stoical disregard for lower back pain are all that's required. What one lacks in the ability to finance say the construction of superior duck accommodation on an exclusive garden pond development can be made up for by toil and imagination.

A tour of the gardens near our school reveals many imaginative lo-cost landscape and design ideas. Some gardens have adopted a culinary theme and feature abandoned fridge freezers or clapped-out cookers. Others have embraced the theme of transport through the ages with interesting arrangements of dismembered bicycles wreathed by brambles, privet hedges screening the skeletal remains of a Ford Sierra and mixed borders of rusting engine parts.

My favourite garden features a group of decapitated gnomes gathered surreally around a derelict wishing well. My least favourite is a bare concrete yard guarded by a dog on steroids that constantly drags its chain through a collection of faeces in various stages of decomposition

Brandon Turner's garden is largely eclectic. Its borders are well stocked with assorted beer cans, broken toys, discarded trainers, an obsolete television set, a mangled umbrella, three dead socks and any number of feral cats he likes to call pets. What raises it above the ordinary is the fact it has a complete three piece suite in it.

No one knows how long it has been there. It was definitely there last winter when it became home to an oddly dysfunctional snow family. It was almost certainly there the previous autumn because one of Brandon's sisters used it as a trampoline to catapult herself into Accident and Emergency (Brandon and his five siblings spend a lot of time in Accident and Emergency).

The rumour is it first appeared two summers ago. There are stories about several police cars arriving at two in the morning to pour cold water on a barbeque that had become a little overheated. Apparently someone's girlfriend was lying on the settee thinking of England when someone else's boyfriend offered to put his sausage in her bap.

From the safety of my lounger I entertain a vague hope that come September the three piece suite in Brandon Turner's garden will have been replaced with more traditional garden furniture. But in my heart of hearts I know it will still be there. It won't affect his learning though. How could it?

And breathe…

10

The driving force

21st August 2015

It is a multisensory experience like no other. Sunlight accentuates every seductive curve of its aerodynamically sculpted body. In an interior as dust free as a microprocessor plant in Silicon Valley volatile organic compounds, off-gassing from new plastic and vinyl, overpower the olfactory system. The advanced eco-intelligent power unit purrs like the cat that got the cream and fell asleep on a duck feather duvet.

Nothing attracts a gathering of salivating males like the arrival of a shiny new car on a quiet suburban avenue. What man could resist that heady mix of eroticised metal and testosterone-fuelled banter? Even men like me, who rarely watch Top Gear and have little practical or technical knowledge of the workings of the internal combustion engine, are drawn irresistibly towards it.

And breathe...

But even as we congratulate Mrs Fraught on her automatic door mirrors with integrated indicators we remember how she lost her previous ones. Those gate posts have a lot to answer for but aren't the main reason her old car looked like a victim of automotive abuse. Keeping a vehicle in pristine condition is easy for mono-tasking old men with little else to do, but for busy working mums faced with motoring's greatest challenges it's a different story. The School Run Derby, the Late-for-work Time Trial and the Supermarket Dash soon sort the girls from the boys.

I smile brightly and advise Mrs Fraught to make the most of her moment of hi-gloss glory. We both know that by darkest December her shiny new car will be colour coded to winter's grime; its stylish interior a repository for assorted sweet wrappers. All working mums (and primary teachers) know that when young children force a person to live life in the fast lane something has to give.

Contrary to popular opinion, teachers' long summer holidays are not a time for coasting along life's byways. These are the days when tired old classrooms are transformed into shiny new ones. It is the season for setting out new learning resources; creating colourful and informative displays; constructing cosy reading corners; neatly labelling exercise books; sticking names on drawers; planning exciting activities for the first week back; and for making unrealistic promises.

How many classrooms not yet tainted by children have inspired these vows? *I do solemnly swear to replace dog-eared displays before their borders sag. I do earnestly pledge to keep on top of marking and pupil record keeping. I hereby attest that I will not leave at the end of the day until (insert any or all of the following) the sink area is clean; the paint cupboard is tidy; reading books are on shelves; pencils are sharpened; iPads are charged; tomorrow's resources are prepared.*

My thoughts are disturbed by a spontaneous ripple of applause as Mrs Fraught drives uncharacteristically slowly over the speed bumps (that have revived the fortunes of our local garage) and away into the distance. It is a signal for men to disperse. Some go away to polish their own cars while others plan a visit to a showroom. I will do neither because I've got far too much work to do in school.

And breathe…

11

Petrolhead Jake revved me up for my DIY duties

12th August 2016

I expect that when car manufacturers design a new vehicle they carry out extensive research to inform the design of an innovative, functional and appealing product that is fit for purpose. That's what the children were required to do in week one of our three-week *Construct a Moving Vehicle* project. In week two they moved on to generating, developing and communicating ideas through discussion, making sketches and producing labelled diagrams.

Week three began with a sigh of relief that the manufacturing process could finally start. Primary students don't always recognise the importance of planning in the technological process. They think you can go straight into full-scale production without a detailed strategy. This is especially true of *kinaesthetic* learners like Jake, whose experience of a *practical curriculum* normally involves cutting out mixed up sentences and re-ordering them.

The idea of *making a car* revved him up like Lewis Hamilton. But when he realised a junior hacksaw was so far down the creative process he'd need to build a telescope out of cardboard tubes to see it coming, he lost control of his emotions and span off at turn one. In order to resolve the situation and to cut a long tantrum short, we gave him a box of resources and left him to his own devices.

While Jake rummaged, his peers formed production companies. They gave themselves names like Velocity Enterprises and Red-hot Racing. A team-work approach allowed them to combine their various skill-sets, which in turn utilised their strengths, eradicated their weaknesses and maximised efficiency. After three weeks (and despite boardroom squabbles, demarcation issues, a management takeover and bouts of shop floor unrest) every group had a product to be proud of.

None more so than Jake, whose vehicle was up and running half way through week one. During week two he added a number of modifications that made his *Firebird* the envy of his peers. By week three his practical skills were in great demand. Where wheels refused to turn on their axles, the solution revolved around Jake. Where propulsion systems failed to propel, Jake was called in to give them a much needed boost.

Now it just so happens that I myself have limited practical skills, so when Mrs Eddison put 'ced*Construct Shelving and Storage System in Utility Room*' (or words to that effect) at the top of my holiday *to-do list,* my impulse was to ignore it. When I later discovered that ignorance wasn't going to lead to marital bliss I remembered Jake and came up with a four-stage plan.

1. Take Pete (a mate with practical skills) for a pint and ask his advice.
2. Accept Pete's offer to view construction site and propose solution.
3. Agree Pete will act as quantity surveyor with authority over acquisition of materials.
4. Assist Pete during building process by locating, passing and holding various tools.

A few days later Pete and I are back in the pub where our conversation has mysteriously veered in the direction of plumbing. Is this a coincidence or is it because the next item on my *to-do list* is '*Mend dripping tap in bathroom*'?

And breathe...

12

Tradesmen wouldn't trade with us

26th August 2011

Coming back from holiday isn't something to look forward to (except for that soggy camping trip to North Wales in 1987). This year, however, we are excited about returning to a shiny new bathroom. See how the sunlight filtered through the venetian blinds makes the chrome taps sparkle and the porcelain sing. See how it makes the tiles dance and the walk-in shower cubicle look too good to walk into.

'It's so beautiful I'm afraid to let you use it,' sighs the wife. She suspects that it's never going to look this good again. Apparently I have a talent for encouraging entropy, which is something to do with the second law of thermodynamics and the scientific fact that everything in the fullness (or where I'm involved shortness) of time decays, crumbles and falls to ruin.

But let's just bask in the moment awhile. For it is truly amazing how a combination of time, effort and craftsmanship can transform a bathroom from something dank and drear – the haunt of numerous malevolent organisms ranging from the micro to the alarmingly macro – into something as hygienically opulent as this.

The creeping, detergent-resistant moulds are vanquished. The bacilli that laughed in the face of bleach are no more. The dust-eating silverfish have been starved out of existence. The woodlice have curled up and died. No dribble of toothpaste stains the sink; nothing sinister lurks beneath the rim of the wall-mounted dual-flush toilet bowl; no pubic hair curls wantonly against the quick-click plug hole.

And the best thing is we didn't get to experience any of the process. We weren't here a week ago when all was chaos. When it was bare walls and naked floorboards; when bits of wire hung down and columns of plaster dust floated up; when a series of swaggering power tools roared and tore and ripped and drilled a frenzied chorus of creativity. The only evidence of the storm preceding this calm is an eye-wateringly large bill.

But a new bathroom comes at a cost that would be entirely prohibitive if builders, like teachers, were required to provide extensive and detailed evidence of the impact of their every action during every aspect of the bathroom fitting process.

Pete the plumber would have had to complete APP grids (Assessing Plumber's Performance) to demonstrate he had achieved age-related expectations in tap connecting, shower fitting and soil pipe technology. Sparky the electrician would have had to traffic light his efforts against the success criteria for wiring up an integrated lighting system, an under-floor heating system and an auto-response extractor fan. Jack (of all trades) would have had to make two positive comments about his workmanship before indicating targets for improvement in one or more of the following areas: sawing, screwing, plastering, nailing, filling, sealing, sticking, tiling, grouting and tea making.

All three would then have had to log their evidence onto a database capable of tracking their group and individual performances over time. This in turn would be used to alert the relevant authorities at *ofbath* should progress towards arbitrarily determined annual targets for raising standards in bathroom fitting appear in danger of being missed.

And finally, just to add a finishing touch, there would have been a requirement to produce a glossy portfolio detailing, through the use of written and photographic evidence, the *Journey of our New Bathroom*. Actually it might have been nice if they'd left the portfolio behind. It would be something to flick through while I'm waiting for nature to take its course.

And breathe...

13

Time, warped

15th August 2014

August is the cruellest month for teachers. Make the most of the brief freedom it brings from school's wearying embrace for it comes at a price. While you enjoy your respite from the clamour of small children; and the mountains of paperwork that crushed your spirits; and the morbid fear that Ofsted might pounce at any moment, dark clouds have already begun to gather. On the not-too-distant horizon September looms.

Right now I'm trying to make the most of the last day of our family holiday by lying in the shade with a cold beer and my kindle edition of *The Unlikely Pilgrimage of Harold Fry*. But unfortunately I'm being pestered by a fly that is repeatedly landing on various parts of my anatomy. I have made several attempts to swat it into fly oblivion but without success.

Sensing my growing annoyance, Brendan from County Cork, who I met at the bar two nights ago, explains the reason I can't hit it. Apparently flies perceive time in a way that is entirely different from the way a teacher on a sun lounger in Lanzarote does.

Until now I had no idea flies even had a perception of time. I thought the only thing they perceived was animal matter in various states of decay. (And my exposed body parts which probably amount to the same thing.) This revelation prompted me to do some Kindle-based research.

In 2013 a team of scientists led by Dr Andrew Jackson from Trinity College Dublin, reported the results of an investigation that explains why flies are difficult to swat. They found that because of their small size and rapid metabolism the insects experienced time at a much slower rate than humans. For example, in the time it will take me to plan and prepare my lessons for the first week back at school, the average house fly will have hatched, pupated, achieved adulthood, lived a life dedicated to satisfying its every carnal desire and been eaten for lunch by a spider.

Even more intriguing than this, the same report goes on to suggest that our experience of time is age related. It passes more slowly for a child than it does for an adult. If this is true, it goes a long way to explain one of life's most enduring mysteries. How does Ryan – like Macavity the Mystery Cat – always manage to be as far away from every crime scene as it's possible to get?

The idea that our perception of time might be flexible raises several fundamental questions. For example, why do weekends disappear in the blink of an eye while Mondays drag on forever? Why do summer holidays hurtle by at the speed of a Boeing 757 on its way to Malaga while the first term back at school grinds forward with all the urgency of a traffic queue on the M25?

These are questions that cry out for further analysis. Preferably while reclining philosophically on a sun lounger and thoughtfully sipping cold beer. But unfortunately it appears time has caught up with me. Already I need to pack my suitcase ready for our flight home.

And breathe…

14

Strike up the band

29th August 2014

As September looms I am plagued by a recurring nightmare. It is one that sees my students return to school even more obsessed with multi-coloured bracelets than they were in July. They are captivated by them to the point where I am invisible. I confiscate them by the handful but more appear. My pockets overflow. My drawers refuse to close. My teacher cupboard bursts open and millions cascade onto the floor.

I had hoped the summer break would kill off the *loom band fad* but its popularity is apparently increasing. Reports that David Beckham and the Duchess of Cambridge have been spotted wearing them don't help; the news that Harry Styles is a big fan is particularly worrying.

For the benefit of anyone who has been in a coma for the last several months, loom bands are tiny, rainbow coloured rubber hoops that can be twisted together – with or without the aid of a specially designed loom – to make fashion accessories such as wrist bands and necklaces. They can also be used to drive teachers insane.

While loom bands boost creativity and promote pattern recognition in maths, their overall contribution to learning is not a positive one. They stimulate time-wasting behaviour in the book corner and seriously inhibit non-chronological report writing. At a more sinister level they have the capacity to inspire acts of antisocial behaviour that include fights, theft and protracted disputes over ownership.

Unfortunately several banning orders towards the end of last term proved ineffective and it occurs to me now that what is needed is an alternative; something equally stimulating but less disruptive of lessons. I cast my mind back to the innocent pastimes of my youth but all I can remember is *clackers*.

For those not at school in the late sixties, clackers comprised of a pair of hard plastic balls attached to either end of a piece of string. The object was to hold the string in the middle and get the balls to clack furiously against each other. This was achieved by means of a rapid up and down motion of the wrist; an action uniquely popular with adolescent boys.

My clackers were eventually confiscated by Mr Kettlewell after they accidentally dropped out of my pocket during a science lesson. 'Any boy caught playing with his clackers in my class will have them permanently removed without the benefit of an anaesthetic,' Mr Kettlewell solemnly announced before cutting my balls off with a craft knife and depositing them in the bin.

Today I am getting ready for the new academic year. This involves emptying my bag of last term's rubbish in order to make room for this term's rubbish. Somewhere near the bottom I unearth a zip lock bag containing several hundred brightly coloured loom bands, two plastic looms and an instruction booklet.

I leaf through the instructions. They are a series of step by step illustrations showing how to produce some basic designs such as the single weave, the squared weave, the starburst, the railroad and the fishtail. On reflection I decide the fishtail pattern looks especially effective. Now I wonder how easy it is to make…

And breathe…

15

Stopping the tide

9th August 2013

In her imagination the King and Queen are on the royal balcony gazing out over their realm. Golden sands stretch like a long forgotten summer down to a rolling blue ocean. Beneath the castle walls valiant knights joust heroically to win the hand of the beautiful princess.

It is a fairytale place until her squabbling brothers blunder into a key section of the northern ramparts and destroy several carefully constructed towers. The big sister's tears and protestations are assuaged by their father, who offers to undertake an emergency rebuilding programme while the kids go off with their mother to buy ice cream.

My wife and I have come to Chapel St Leonards for the day, a Lincolnshire seaside village on the East Coast of England. This is where my family spent its annual holidays during the late fifties and early sixties. We stayed in one of hundreds of caravans that still shelter behind sea defences built to protect local communities from flooding and the nation from Nazi domination.

On the seaward side of this defiant concrete wall is a mile-long stretch of beach where I used to build my own sandcastles. Today my creative energy will mainly be confined to keeping sand out of my cheese and beetroot sandwiches. Having erected my lightweight multi-functional reclining lounger and beach chair I settle back to watch the families at play.

You can have lots of fun with a bucket and spade and endless supplies of sand. I once got my dad to bury me up to the neck. 'Will you dig me out now, Dad?' I asked after about three minutes. Panic set in when no reply came from behind the stripy windbreak. 'Dad, what if the tide comes in?... Dad, are you still there?'

How satisfying it is to cast the dead weight of a year's worth of detailed planning and assessments into the abyss of a computer hard drive; submerged for all time in a folder marked 2012–13. September is still beyond the horizon. At last I can get my breath back and relax. The pressure to raise attainment ebbs away. Brandon's tantrums already look like minor squalls. Mal de lesson observation no longer makes my stomach churn.

From the moment it begins the school year is a race against time to put every new practice and strategy into place. On the flimsiest of foundations we construct alternative ways of working that we hope will maximise results and help us achieve the unachievable. To de-motivate us in the right direction we are set targets that are more challenging than the one where William Tell stuck an apple on his son's head and told him to stand very, very still.

But standing still is something teachers can't contemplate, for if the pace drops marginally below frenetic you get dragged out to sea by the undertow of all the things you didn't get done. The job has never been more demanding than it is now: high stakes, high visibility and greedy for evidence. And all you can do when the tide is against you and the vastness of the ocean seeks to swallow you up is thrash around like crazy and pray you don't go under.

I must have fallen asleep because when I open my eyes it is late afternoon and the beach is almost deserted. The families have packed up their dreams and left to go to Sue's Seaside Chippy or the bright lights of Bibby's amusement arcade. The few castles that survived the day's exertions have been abandoned to their fates. The wind is changing. The tide is already on the turn.

A short plenary

In keeping with the theme of being a classroom teacher, I thought I should end these tales with a short plenary. However, as I'm not exactly sure what a plenary is (in much the same way that I'm not sure how to teach year six children to expand a noun phrase by adding or modifying adjectives, nouns and prepositional phrases) I'll just say a word of thanks and/or apologies to all those who inspired them.

In no particular order these include children, parents, colleagues, family members, TES staff (especially former Deputy Editor Ed Dorrell) and Ms Boudicca (she knows who she is) who insists on dragging this old septuagenarian back into her school every year in order to teach drama and put together the school production.

This book is printed on paper from sustainable sources managed under the Forest Stewardship Council (FSC) scheme.

It has been printed in the UK to reduce transportation miles and their impact upon the environment.

For every new title that Troubador publishes, we plant a tree to offset CO_2, partnering with the More Trees scheme.

MORE TREES
LET'S PLANT A BILLION TREES

For more about how Troubador offsets its environmental impact, see www.troubador.co.uk/sustainability-and-community